FUN PARTY GAMES

FUN PARTY GAMES
FOR ALL AGES
AND
ALL OCCASIONS

by Bernice Hogan

BBH

BAKER BOOK HOUSE
Grand Rapids, Michigan

Copyright 1969 by
Hewitt House, A Division of
Fleming H. Revell Company
Reprinted 1975 by
Baker Book House
ISBN: 0-8010-4111-2
Library of Congress Catalog Card Number: 71-85316

Second printing, July 1978

Printed in the United States of America

To My Husband

Acknowledgments

Acknowledgment is gratefully made for permission to include selections in this publication to:

Japan Air Lines for material from *Japan Air Lines Gourmet Guide to the Orient* and *Culinary Arts* in the Oriental Wingding

Kikkoman International, Inc. and Rachel Carr for material from *"The Japanese Way With Food and Flowers"* and the arrangement *"Rustic Simplicity."*

Kikkoman International, Inc. for the recipes "Spareribs Kyoto," "Tuna Pilaf," "Lamb Kabobs," "Kikko-Cream Vegetable Sauce" and "Kikko-Burgers," from *The Japanese Way With Food and Flowers.*

Tea Council of the U.S.A., Inc. for recipes "Open House Punch," "Instant Tea Punch" and "Hot Spiced Tea" from *What You Should Know About Tea.*

Joan Rowland, *Fun and Festival From the Middle East,* 1958, Friendship Press in Persian Garden Party.

To Ideal Toy Corporation of New York, and Parker Brothers, Inc. of Salem, Massachusetts for games used in the "Last Chance Party."

Bernice Hogan, "Games by the Mile," *Hearthstone,* Christian Board of Publications, July-August, 1968.

Bernice Hogan, "Plans for New Year's Eve at the Church" (Theme:

A Musical Note) LEADER GUIDEBOOK, David C. Cook Publishing Company.

"Peanut Cookies," "Leaning Tower," "Crunchy Picnic Candy," "Skillet Corn Bread," and "Sour Cream Pancakes" are recipes from QUAKER QUOTES, The Quaker Oats Company.

"Lasagne," "Baked Polenta" and "Pizza" are recipes issued by the Knox County Homemakers Extension Association in cooperation with the University of Illinois.

"Rose Paperweight" from Shabonee Girl Scout Council, Inc. of the Girl Scouts of America, Moline, Illinois.

Anita White and the Library Club of Abingdon High School, Abingdon, Illinois for parties and ideas in "High School Corridors" with particular suggestions from Susie Lewis, Ruth Ann Morby, Connie Boone, and Susan Batson.

Lucile Ahern for the recipes, "Chinese Chicken" and "Chicken Mousse"; Susan Abernethy for "Raw Apple Cake"; Laura Finch for "Dark Fruit Cake"; Susy Fluegel for psychedelic art ideas; John and Margery Newman for the "Charivari" experiences from The Abingdon *Argus;* and Ginny McGlosson for "Carrot Cake," "Squash Casserole," "Valentine Strawberry Cake" and "Christmount" ideas; and Marieva Bradbury for "Coney Dogs."

"Svivon," a Hebrew game, Children's Program Publications, by permission of the American Friends Service Committee.

Preface

Whether you have met Bernice Hogan at a party or in a book, you know she effervesces with ideas for creating fun and inspiring people with novel party ideas. The purpose of this book is to bring people together for good times and to produce instant fun for people already gathered together.

A very different approach to folks and fun provides delightful reading. The themes of Persian nights and French twilights glitter with exciting foods and exotic decor, but the hillbilly and the hot dog are not forsaken.

The fun is for anybody; the parties are for everybody; the games are for all. There are simple activities for several children and elaborate plans for a crowd of adults. There are teen-age happenings and nursing home frolics.

Mrs. Hogan has created a handy reference work of sparkling ideas. It is a fun book to read *and* a fun book to use.

THE PUBLISHERS

The Route to FUN PARTY GAMES

 to assure success for your party is to plan carefully where you want to go (what kind of party), and who you want to travel with you (your guests).

 require the road markers to be checked: date of party, time and whether or not it interferes with the PTA Bazaar, the Bowling Banquet, or Aunt Mehitabel and Uncle Charlie's Golden Wedding Anniversary.

 to imagination while packing. Produce clever invitations and amusing entertainment.

 may indicate a need to rev the motor or change the directional signals to keep the party moving.

 for fascinating scenery unless you have created special decorations for the route.

 for food that's tempting.

 for unusual ideas to entertain your guests.

Table of Directions and Contents

1 Young Roads

Paper Doll Parade

Little girls, ages five to nine years, usually find paper dolls perennially delightful, so a party on this theme has a built-in success feature.

The girls are not encouraged to bring their own paper dolls. The necks have a way of bending and the ankles breaking, so that after a party session there's apt to be built-in gloom instead of fun, if a favorite paper gal has been reduced to scraps.

INVITATIONS: A paper doll, what else?

This can be adequately cut from a catalog of girls' or women's clothing and be reinforced with white poster board on the back to give durability to the doll as well as a space for the invitation:

> Howdy, howdy! Come and see
> How does your paper doll grow,
> With curl-free hair and ponytail
> And boy friends all in a row!

You'll need to cut out dolls with arms not too widespread so they can fit in the standard business envelope. Perhaps the young party hostess may prefer to deliver the doll invitations in person, if her guests are in the same neighborhood. They should not be delivered at school unless every girl in the class is to receive one.

DECORATIONS: Paper dolls galore in all shapes and a dozen sizes. One particularly tall, slim, svelte gal might be made from

17

poster board and pose against a cardboard stand by the front door
to welcome guests to the Parade Party.

Other paper boy and girl friends might be sitting on lamp
shades, picture frames, peering over chandeliers with some as
small as key hole covers.

I think I would choose pink as a basic color for the decorations
(such as the streamers you may twist to dangle paper dolls from)
but any pastel color would be appropriate. Ask your own "doll"
hostess whether she prefers violet, yellow, or mint green.

A paper doll with a frilly expanding paper skirt makes a delightful table centerpiece, and you can choose solid pastel paper
tablecloth and napkins to match or contrast.

FASHION PARADE

FUN: The essential ingredient of a Paper Doll Parade Party is
most certainly a fashion show, so sharpen your scissors and wits
and gather up some of the following:

   Paper dolls (from the dime store) Try to keep the dolls of
      fairly similar size. The less expensive books may have more
      dolls, but the cardboard may be less strong and need addi-
      tional reinforcement.
   Foil paper (possibly salvaged from Christmas or birthday
      gifts)
   Tissue paper, white glue, sequins, small scraps of lace, cloth,
      ribbon, scissors, tiny buttons (to be glued on outfits, if
      desired), pencils, crayons and whatever other notion knick-
      knacks you may conjure up.

With this equipment, plus any other your sewing box or art kit
may reveal, each girl may dress her paper doll in a parade costume.

Allow twenty minutes time limit and give the girls time warnings
every five minutes so they can plan their lace pasting and fringe
cutting.

For the Parade itself, have each girl carry her doll about the
room, model fashion. The girls may vote for their own favorite
choice of the "Best-Dressed Paper Doll of the Year," or else some

neighborhood mothers may make the decision. If more than one prize is available—and most girls are more delighted with lots of smaller prizes rather than one big award—you might give awards of at least prize ribbons in the following categories:

Prettiest
Funniest
Most Original
Largest Variety of Materials Used in Costume

DOLL HOPPING RELAY

Have the girls line up in three even teams for a Doll Hopping Relay. If they seem to have difficulty dividing themselves into teams, count off, "One, two, three; one, two, three; one, two, three, etc." Then place all numbers one's against the east wall, number two's in the center and perhaps number three's against the west wall.

With paper doll in one hand and paper doll costumes in the other (either the ones from the Parade or an outfit from the cut-out books) the first girl in each of the three lines must hop from the starting line to the opposite end of the room, dress her paper doll, then undress her, leaving the clothes in a pile. Each girl then hops back to the end of her team and the new girl in first place starts hopping off for the dressing corner. The team to finish hopping and outfitting first wins some token prizes such as yo-yos or small purse mirrors. (Set a minimum number of paper clothing pieces as a requirement for each contestant to carry.)

PAPER-PEOPLE SCRAMBLE

Before the party, the hostess might hide at least a hundred small paper dolls in many strange places in the room where the Parade is to take place, and then at a given gala moment of the party, all the girls can scramble to hunt for as many dolls as possible.

Take the dolls either from catalogs or make the long folded accordion-shaped dolls cut apart. These are easy (see illustration) and may be made from a single pastel color to make all the paper dolls in the scramble the same size and color.

An inexpensive book of paper dolls might reward the gal finding the most paper people.

FAVORS: A gingerbread girl in transparent bag for each child for easy carry-home

OR

An award insignia, complete with two-inch-wide ribbon and a round cardboard medal with pin attached announcing: I'M A PAPER-PEOPLE PERSON! or: I'M A PAPER-PEOPLE FAN!

FOOD: Butterscotch sundaes with sugar cookies. The gimmick is that the cookies have faces painted on with egg yolk and food coloring, or features outlined by circle candies and stuck on with confectioner's sugar frosting. Well, cookie people if not paper people!

Elephant Wobble

This sounds as if it might be the name of the latest dance sensation, or at the very least, a spectacular cracker snack discovery; however, if you elephant wobble well, you may become a party-giver sensational in the eyes of your son, daughter or favorite grandchild.

This can be adapted for a birthday party, a Cub Scout or Brownie get-together or even broadened to include the entire homeroom, if you're a class mother or a bushed and bedraggled teacher. (Now, teachers, don't be offended, because I teach in the elementary school also, and am very bushed and very, very bedraggled, too, when the last half-hour of the last school day finally arrives). It's "party time" which the children have been anticipating and wheedling for during the last eight and one-half months!

In fact, I suspect that the only reason I am now brave enough to write about such a party, is that it is midsummer and six weeks on either side of class parties!

Let me share how one teacher encouraged good behavior for a good many days prior to "party time." For each day that the pupils were well behaved, they were allowed to add to the blackboard one letter of the party theme and if the words were completed by the party date, the celebration could come off. For example, a week before the party, the words on the blackboard might now say: ELEPHANT W – – – – – . Mothers might also use this sort of encouragement on the kitchen bulletin board!

INVITATIONS: A wobbling elephant would make a perfect picture for the front of your invitations. If art is not your forté, however, scour the dime and drug stores for a traceable card or coloring book picture that you can cut and outline. Pink construction paper for invitations with gray elephants wobbling around on top strikes a garish note for me, but you may paste your elephants on whatever pleases your own children (no, please—not the bathtub or the principal's desk!).

DECORATIONS: You may be able to wangle some wobbly elephant pictures from your friendly supermarket manager. Frequently peanut butter, cereal flakes or animal cracker displays have an at least slightly wobbled elephant display.

Otherwise, you might enlarge the invitation elephant to a large sheet of poster board and stand the result in your picture window or front door. If this seems like too much work, just forget about the whole idea and hang up a few balloons and a string of peanuts, instead.

This provides refreshments, if the children get hungry before you do; and if you run out of game ideas, the boys and girls will be delighted to see who can make the largest pile of scrunchy shell pieces on your wall-to-wall carpeting!

FUN: As the children arrive, give instructions that whenever they walk around during the party, they must wobble like an elephant; that is, walk bent over with arms swinging together like a trunk in front of them. There is a double purpose for this: besides being a fun walk, think of all the wrestling, pulling, elbowing temptations you will eliminate.

The next two game suggestions came from a training session of the Shabonee Girl Scout Council, Inc. of the Girl Scouts of America, so they've been well tested on girls and leaders.

ELEPHANT "IT"

The group sits or stands in a circle, close enough to touch each other, since all the action and movement is done in groups of three.

One person is in center as Elephant "it." This "it" looks at the circle and turns around slowly, then calls "Elephant!" and points to one person.

The person to whom "it" points must immediately place both fists to nose to form the trunk while the persons on the left and right must immediately place their hands to this person's head to make big ears.

"It" then chooses the slowest one of the three who made up the "Elephant" to take her place and be in the center and the game continues. If "it" cannot decide which one was the last, she points to another "elephant."

After the group is familiar with this game, the rules may be made more difficult by adding other animals and alternating them. For example "Raccoon" might be called out with the center person making a mask with fingers around eyes and the person on either side making little ears on him or her with cupped hands.

For older boys and girls, if "Rabbit" is also added, the group must stand to include this portion of the game. When "it" calls "Rabbit," both hands of the center person are put to back to form a tail while two tall ears are formed by persons on the left and right.

Real expert players use all three animals at one time. "It" must be sure to call out the proper animals however. Large groups can be divided into circles or else two or three "its" are used.

ELEPHANT AND THE SPIDER WEB

This is another delightful circle game with the first elephant wobbling around the center, bent down with arms hanging as a trunk while the group chants:

> An elephant began to play
> Upon a spider web one day
> He had such great, delightful fun,
> He called for another elephant to come:
> "Hey! Elephant!"

At the last line, the center elephant backs up to someone, and reaching back with one arm between his legs, grabs one hand or trunk of the person (elephant) wobbling behind him (see illustration).

The song is repeated and both bent-over wobbling elephants back up to add another elephant to the line, with the second elephant holding to the front elephant's left hand or trunk and putting his left hand between his legs to grasp the third elephant's trunk (right hand).

The song is again repeated with still another elephant added to the line. The entire procedure can be repeated till the entire circle is included in the elephant wobble line, or halted when utter bedlam takes over.

PEANUT SCRAMBLE

Peanuts in their shells make marvelous items for scrambling, provided you are of the scrambling age rather than the cleaning-up-afterwards generation. If you have a barn, a messy backyard, or lots of fortitude and enthusiasm for peanut shells, it's a nice elephant party idea.

If you scatter the peanuts over a wide area out-of-doors, this might guarantee an entire ten-minute quiet time for you to dish up the ice cream!

Another possibility for those hostesses with energy beyond the party duty, is to spray the peanut shells with gold paint for real "treasure-nut hunting."

FAVORS:

A box of animal crackers for each guest

OR

A nut cup filled with candy circus peanuts

OR

A nut cup filled with nuts

OR

Peanuts in the shell, sprayed gold, and strung on a string as necklace or golden Hawaiian lei

FOOD: Brownies with lots of frosting and vanilla ice cream with lots of nuts!

Fun By the Mile

This can hardly be called a party. We may even be stretching a point in calling it "Fun" by the Mile, but there does come a time in almost every family when traveling is a Must for fun or business, relatives or pleasure. This is written to lessen travel tedium and in the hope that your on-the-road experiences will be better than ours have been in fifteen years of piling our offspring into the back seat.

INVITATIONS: None, of course, just a warning. Traveling with young children *can* be a series of whining, crying, pushing shoving explosions punctuated with irregular yells! To prevent frazzled nerves, and to give one's traveling the semblance of fun and order, try some advanced preparations.

DECORATIONS: For this fun-creating relay, let's term the stuff you take along more accurately as Equipment, but if you feel optimistic, keep thinking of it as Car Decorations.

Consider stocking the glove compartment, unless it's like ours, already overflowing with half-used paper napkins, paper containers spilling salt, and plastic straws that match non-existent drinks. If the glove compartment and trunk are over-stuffed, then make a THIS IS NOT A LITTER BAG.

Small notebook for each child—the 3″ x 5″ size or smaller
Stubby pencils—the kind they put in church pews

Marking pencils—these are crayon substitutes. Have you ever taken crayons on a summer trip, like we have, and left them in the sun on the back seat? Such a mottled, melted mess you could not otherwise imagine!

No scissors—even blunt ones can stab well, and besides, who wants to clean up clippings at the end of the day?

Card games like "Lotto," "Old Maids!" "Authors" or some of the newer ones from your local dime store.

Traveling games packaged for just such harassed parents as all of us are.

Puzzles—(not the jig-saw kind) metal ones to be undone or wooden squares, balls or elephants that are supposed to be unlocked, then put together again. Hooray for the missing pieces!

Checkers or Chess—the small, inexpensive kind for traveling. Some have slots on the board into which the pieces can be pushed for mountain roads and hairpin passes.

FUN: Ration out the equipment and your ideas. If you've used up your ideas the first hour, and 1600 miles remain to be covered before you reach home again, it's going to be a long, hot summer. Consider *Riddles*.

Remember the kind that we grew up with: "What is black and white and red (read) all over?" In our day, the answer was, "A newspaper," but the children in the back seat will probably answer: "A sunburned zebra."

For preschool children, make up riddles about things you can see from the car window:

> You can see me now
>   when you look up high,
> I'm sometimes blue
> and I am the —— (sky).

Songs

Songs are always good fillers, and the choice of subject matter depends upon the ages of your children. If everyone can at least partially carry a tune, try a round like "White Coral Bells," "Three Blind Mice" or "Row, Row, Row Your Boat."

Brownies or Cub Scouts will have songs from their own scouting programs, and if boys and girls have been to camp, there's no limit to "John Jacob Jingleheimer Smith," "The Grand Old Duke of York" and "On Top of Old Smoky."

MYSTERY STORIES

Mystery stories are always popular. Start with a particularly weird tale of "a dark midnight in an old cemetery, when suddenly from behind a cracking tombstone, there arose . . ."

Leave the story at some exciting, suspenseful point and ask someone else to add a few more lines of spine-tingling drama. That person then stops at an exciting spot and the story goes on to the next player, till all are completely mystified and un-storied.

The old, old game of "I'm going on a trip and I'm going to take an *A*pple, *B*asket, . . . ," using each letter of the alphabet, with everyone adding a commodity, but having to repeat all the alphabetical items previously mentioned, can be altered. Use only food or only flowers or only animals for the letters. With the last category, you might say, "I'm going to Kalama*z*oo and I'm going to take an *A*ntelope, *B*illy-goat, *C*aribou, *D*ragon, etc."

LICENSE PLATES

Now, have the children use those stubby pencils and notebooks stowed in that non-litter bag. Each one lists as many different license plates as he can see and recognize. Rest stops add half a dozen entries. You can decide on the rules—whether or not license plates *not* on the move are valid! You'll probably be voted down whatever your decision.

SIGN GAMES

Some favorite car diversions utilize the well-known sign games in which each person finds words in alphabetical order from sign-boards along the highway. This works best with two players, one

using each side of the car or road.   Make it a trifle more difficult
by having players search for words using the alphabet in reverse!

You can count anything on a trip, depending upon the section
of the country: deer, stop signs, Fords, mountains, red trucks,
railroad crossings, cows and creeks.   If you want to count a
number of things at one time, devise some sort of point value for
the items as:

1 brown cow	5 points
1 1969 Chevrolet	3 points
1 man in red shirt	4 points
1 gas station selling pop where Pop won't stop	1 point
6 sheep	10 points
3 trucks all at one time	4 points
1 ice cream stand where you *do* stop	10 points and time to end the game!

The one with the most points at the stand wins—or the first
one that reaches fifty points.

A variation of this same game which keeps you on the alert
for road signs and scenery highlights is to make a list for each of
the players (both adults and children can enjoy this).   Have the
same items on each list, but put them in a different order.   Each
person must find the clues in the order listed, so if a black cow
is seen when the game begins, probably only one player can get
credit and go on to the second requirement.

Here are some possible lists:

1. Black cow	1. Freight train
2. Green and white license plate	2. Man with necktie on
3. Stump of tree	3. Black cow
4. Black pick-up truck	4. Woman carrying baby
5. Moving van	5. Green and white license plate
6. Freight train	6. Restaurant
7. Root beer stand	7. Moving van

8. Railroad crossing
9. Restaurant
10. Woman carrying baby
11. Man with necktie on
12. Picnic table

8. Railroad crossing
9. Black pick-up truck
10. Root beer stand
11. Picnic table
12. Stump of tree

Mix the order up in as many lists as you have players. Better set a time limit on this since probably no one will get through the entire list.

"Auto-Spy"

"AUTO-SPY" is a favorite game with many children. The object is to discover through questions what "it" has picked as a secret chosen article. My own children play this while waiting for their minister father to make hospital calls. Then they choose items outside the car around the parking lot, but if you're whizzing down the highway, you'd better choose something *inside*. "It" begins by saying, "I spy something that begins with 'l.' "

After several wrong guesses from the others in the car, he may add another clue like, "It is red." Someone may then discover that "it" has chosen the small red light on the dashboard. The discoverer then becomes "it" and picks out an ever-more-difficult auto item.

Odds and Games

"Tic-tac-toe" on those serviceable notebooks with the stubby pencils is always good for at least eighteen miles. Remember, too, the old pencil and paper game of "Hangman" where dashes are marked out according to the number of letters in the chosen hidden words.

—————— —— ———— (Fourth of July)

OR

———————— ————————
(Abraham Lincoln)

Players give a possible letter, which is filled in on the proper dashes, if it is in the words. A correct letter wins another turn, but an incorrect letter (that is, one not in the words) gets a head drawn for the hangman's noose. If the body is filled in as the result of improper guesses, arm by arm and leg by leg, the game is lost and the same person gets to dash out another word. If the player guesses the word, however, it becomes his turn to play hangman.

FOOD AND FAVORS: Is it time now for a song to break the monotony of the trip? If not, it's surely time for a rest stop. It's advisable to stretch and wash up every two hours on a long trip.

A piece of fresh fruit for everyone gives renewed energy. Pack a good supply before leaving home, for you may find apples or oranges inaccessible at your rest stop, or else extremely expensive.

The rule is that everyone has to get out at all stops, even if it's just for stretching legs and arms near the car. More states are constructing more and more rest areas along the highway, because they know such places contribute to safety and the enjoyment of the tourist.

An occasional stop at a gift shop for favors or souvenirs or just looking can be fun, but make most of the pauses in the out-of-doors where a quick game of tag can be in order or some hurried races, scrambles or somersaults. Nothing like a cartwheel to clear the mind!

LAST LAP IDEAS: Back in the car, try to stagger the seating arrangement, so that everybody gets a window seat sooner or later. Encourage the children to use their notebooks as log books, keeping track of what time they left where and arrived when, as well as the number of miles covered and the towns passed through.

It will be useful for older children to keep track of the costs of traveling:

How much money spent for how many gallons of gas?
Cost of oil change.
Toll-road fees. Have children figure out how much per mile the toll amounts to.

Children, as well as adults, are interested in money. They think in terms of a dime for a soft drink at home, but with a budget and a log book they may discover that on the road this same drink costs twenty-five cents, and that with five persons in the car, an inexpensive soft drink amounts to $1.25. If the children have their own travel allowances, they'll be much less inclined to want to stop so often for ice cream cones!

Party to Read By

As a remedial reading teacher in the Abingdon Grade School, each week I meet with eighty-four boys and girls who have problems in reading. Across the country there are thousands of pupils with reading difficulties so severe that the young people cannot learn adequately in science, history or other subjects which require the reading of assignments in text or reference books.

One reason for the difficulty may be that the pupil doesn't *like* to read. He or she may never have had pleasant experiences with books. It is in a party such as this that the young child may discover for the first time that reading *can* be fun. And easy! And not something only to be done in a classroom!

This is a party in which games are played which use reading skills. You may not want to use every game at one party, but be aware that reading can be fun and that boys and girls learn more ably when *they* think it's fun. At an informal gathering of children, play one of these games; during a family evening, use a reading activity. You don't have to call a celebration a *Reading Party,* but you can slip one of these "fun to read" projects into a birthday party or even a Hobo Cook-Out.

Don't be afraid to help children discover the fun in reading!

INVITATIONS: As has been suggested, you may want to fit some reading games into a birthday party or Valentine get-together, and soft-pedal the whole emphasis that fun can be for reading improvement.

On the other hand, you may wish to jump into the middle of

33

the whole matter and have a Book Party with everyone coming as a character in a favorite story—anything from *Sleeping Beauty* to the witch in *Hansel and Gretel,* or *Robinson Crusoe* or even a current comic strip hero.

DECORATIONS: If the reading fun is just to be interspersed in an Astronaut Party or a Treasure Hunt, follow the original theme for your hangings and drapings.

If this is to be a Book Party, however, make some cardboard dolls with styrofoam heads and book-cover bodies to perch on table and piano, or with the foam heads cut in half, to stroll casually across the bulletin board or front door.

Make a poster saying "It's FUN to read!" with boys and girls really having fun with books on it.

On a large sheet of poster board, draw horizontal lines for bookshelves, and cut out strips to represent book covers and paste them on the shelves. Let the children, as they arrive, print on the covers the names of as many books as they can remember that they have read. If one child can remember five titles, he'll write the title of each on five jacket ends.

Make name tags before the party saying in large block letters: "The book I like best is ————." When each child arrives, ask him to fill in the blank if he is in third grade or higher. You'll need to ask first-graders what *story* they like best and print the name yourself, or maybe draw a hasty picture of "The Three Bears" or "The Ugly Duckling."

FUN: Read, or much better, *tell* a story to the boys and girls present. If you've lost track of what particularly interests this age group, ask the children's librarian or a teacher in the elementary school. These informed people may be able to direct you to some very exciting children's material.

Puppet Show

Draft two teen-agers into putting on a puppet show using one of the children's favorite stories as the basis for the play. Regular puppets can be used, or if these are not available, simply make some from socks with the toes stuffed with old nylons for the head. Paper-bag puppets are very easy and inexpensive. Use small bags, possibly from the bakery, and draw a face on what would be the bottom of the bag. Cut holes in the sides for your thumb and ring finger to go through as arms, with your pointing and middle fingers in the head so the character can nod or bend fairly naturally.

If you don't want to fashion a tall cardboard stage, have the actors stoop behind a table with the puppets being manipulated on the table top. Be sure to cover the table with a long cloth so the puppeteers can't be seen sitting underneath!

TOP BANANA!

Each member of two teams is given three different words printed on yellow construction paper in the shapes of individual bananas.

The hostess has already prepared matching bananas for herself which either she or "it" or "teacher" will hold up at the designated time. If there are six boys and girls on each team, she will have had to prepare thirty-six banana words for herself and thirty-six to be divided among the two teams.

The words used will depend upon the grade level of the children who are playing. The hostess may take the words either from a book of this same grade, from the children's spelling list, or from a vocabulary list suggested by one of the elementary teachers of that age group.

As the game begins, the hostess, or someone who has been chosen "it" or "teacher," holds up a banana with a word printed on it.

When a player's banana word matches the word held up, the boy or girl runs forward and can claim the second banana from the hostess, *if* he can read the word.

He must turn in his banana word, if he cannot identify it. The words, in banana form, continue to be held up till all have been accounted for. Each team then totals the number of bananas it has and the winning team members might each receive a real banana or a candy bar each for their "top banana" reading.

HATS OFF!

Give each child a paper plate which he can use as a hat. If you have lots of time, allow the guests to draw designs on their hats or color them as they choose.

As the game begins, have all the children stand in a circle as you call out pairs of words. If the two words you call are rhyming words, the children put on their hats, but if the words do not rhyme, they remain hatless.

As the game progresses, you may read the words more quickly. This is an "all for fun" game, with no one dropping out when an error is made. Perhaps each child can receive a lollipop for participating.

Here are some rhyming words. (You can easily add your own which do not rhyme)

noon	moon
cat	sat
boat	goat
ball	tall
call	fall
cat	rat
mat	hat
pig	dig

You can repeat the game "Hats Off!" later in the party by having the children stand in a line for this variation and put on their hats whenever two words are given with the same beginning sound. Your calling might go like this:

corn	cat	(Hats on)
dig	dog	(Hats on)
ball	doll	(Hats off)

man	make	(Hats on)
pig	dig	(Hats off)
boat	dog	(Hats off)
coat	doll	(Hats off)
ball	bat	(Hats on)
boy	book	(Hats on)
girl	boy	(Hats off)
girl	good	(Hats on)

The hats will make a take home souvenir for each child. Maybe he'll think of it as his "reading hat" or "thinking cap!"

READ AND SHARE

If your guests are in at least third grade, before the party you can clip out a number of jokes, quotations and short poems. Paste each one to a bright piece of construction paper, and then let each child scramble to find one item he or she would like to read to the rest of the guests. You can even use the greetings on birthday cards, if they're appropriate.

Don't make any selection very long, but give every child a chance to "read and share," *if* he wants to do so. Don't push nor insist that the very shy youngster participate; perhaps he will when the others have completed theirs.

FAVORS: A bookmark made either from felt or construction paper would be a most obvious but most satisfactory take-home favor. Six to eight year-olds would enjoy making their own; cut out light cardboard strips and give them a good choice of stickers and gold paper for decoration.

FOOD: For children a party is not a party at all unless there is ice cream and cake. Make the cake easier for you to serve and the children to eat by having cupcakes. These can have letters of the alphabet printed on them with contrasting frosting, and one cupcake might even conceal a dime well-wrapped in foil.

Vanilla ice cream is probably the safest choice for you, and, for your own piece of mind, don't give anybody a chance to choose among chocolate, peach and butter-pecan!

Octopus Party

With its eight tentacles, the octopus has four times as many arms
with which to enjoy a party as has its human counterpart. Very
simply then, an Octopus party ought to be four times as much fun
as any other kind!

Imagination is the key, with splashy pictures, lots of food and
a contagious, bubbly enthusiasm as important as arms to the whole
affair.

This can readily be adapted for a birthday party. Birthday
affairs ought to have themes, too, you know rather than merely to
depend on the traditional candles and cake for their spirit.

An octopus taxes your imagination because a live octopus is
actually not a very appealing creature; but *your* responsibility is
to make him party-funny—a humorous character with four times
as many possibilities as any usual body.

If it's summer, you can take the party out-of-doors, though
you'll then need to reinforce your octopi with stiffer cardboard
or wooden slat backings. If it's Christmas, make your octopus in
red and green, or for Valentine's Day stick to red.

Now where else could you find such a versatile animal for a
party!

INVITATIONS: With black marking pen on stark white tagboard draw a handsome black octopus—the size you would like
for your invitations. Probably the invitations should be square
and of a size for which you've already found correct-fitting envelopes. There is almost nothing more frustrating than to have

made absolutely handsome, beautiful, stylish and mod invitations and then discover there is nothing they slip into for mailing. Look first for the envelopes and *then* draw the eight tentacles to fit the corners!

Your party octopus ought to have a cartoon quality, a humorous smirk to his countenance. You might attempt to achieve this appearance by making quite giant eyes with no mouth or nose at all to mar his huge "lookers."

DECORATIONS: A large packing box from a neighborhood store, perhaps one that had contained a refrigerator or some other large appliance, would yield four marvelously large octopi, one on each side of the box. With black enamel, draw the outline of this party creature, perhaps with red eyes and even red ribbons on each tentacle, so he will be well dressed for a festive occasion. You might even decide to make the octopus a "she" instead; or, you could have a "he" and "she" octopus walking tentacle in tentacle up the party room wall.

Take a kitchen stool and top it with the fanciest satin pillow you own for the throne of the Octopus King. If you want other than a cardboard King Octopus, you can make one easily from rug yarn on a twenty-inch cardboard frame, just as you make the smaller yarn creatures in the Favors section of this party. This large yarn animal can be an attractive bed decoration later, and perhaps a gift for the honored child, if this is a birthday party.

You might make the body of one octopus from cardboard and his tentacles from string or rope. Hang him on a chandelier and make his tentacles long enough to dangle in the faces of guests when they walk under him.

Happy octopus making!

ODD OCTOPUS

FUN: This is a variation of the old favorite "Poor Pussy." Have all your guests gather in a circle and be seated. One person is the Odd Octopus.

The Octopus waddles over in front of a seated player and gurgles, rolls his eyes, makes faces and, in as many ways as possi-

ḷake that guest laugh. The player must pat the head
ṣopus and add, "Odd Octopus," three times without

, guest is successful and does not laugh, Odd Octopus goes
on to another player and gurgles, but must not speak. If this
guest laughs, he also becomes an Odd Octopus and tries to make
other persons laugh.

The game continues until everyone at the party has become an
Odd Octopus. The last person to laugh is the winner and might
receive a joke book as a prize.

If the game continues too long, you may ring a bell and all
those who have not yet been made an Odd Octopus are the win-
ners.

OCTOPUS IN THE NET

This is a lively game and well adapted for ten or twelve active
guests. Let everyone join hands in a circle which will be a "net"
for this game, with one person as the Octopus inside the net.

Blow a whistle to begin. Now the Octopus runs to any spot in
the net and tries to break out by crawling under arms or legs or
by stepping over or breaking through hands.

If and when the Octopus breaks out of the net, the net breaks
and everyone tries to catch him. The person who catches him
becomes the new Octopus and the net forms tightly again.

FISHY RHYME KNOWLEDGE

Here are some nursery rhyme reminders. Give out pencils and
papers with the following questions printed on them. Don't forget
to omit the answers when you prepare this fishy test.

1. What did Simple Simon try to catch in his mother's pail?
   (whale)
2. Who went to sea in a tub? (the butcher, the baker, the
   candlestick maker)
3. What will Bobby Shaftoe do when he comes back from
   sea? (marry me)

4. Hey-diddle-diddle, where did the cow jump?   (over the moon)

5. What did Old King Cole want besides his fiddlers three? (his pipe and his bowl)

6. Did Humpty Dumpty sit on a brick wall?   (nobody knows —do you?)

7. Why was Mary quite contrary?   (you might consider the funniest answer to this question as the correct one)

8. Did Jack and Jill go up the hill to fill their pail with water?   (no, to *fetch* a pail of water)

9. Do you think Bo-Peep's sheep will bring anything with them when they come home?   (yes, probably their tails wagging behind them)

10. Where were the cows when Little Boy Blue blew his horn? (the cows were in the corn)

11. How many children did Old Mother Hubbard have?   (none that we know of—just a dog, it was The Old Woman Who Lived in a Shoe who had all those children)

12. Who put poor Pussy in the well?   (little Johnny Green, we've always been told)

FAVORS: If you have lots of patience and a good bit of time, you can make each one of your guests a cute yarn octopus. It takes about forty-five minutes to complete one of the creatures. Maybe you could line up your family to help and make them asembly-line style to cut down on that time.

Here is what you'll need:

quite a good bit of colored yarn for the main body of the octopus, enough to go around a 5 inch cardboard 24 times

1 or 2 yards of contrasting yarn for tying tentacles, necktie, etc.

2 white buttons for eyes

This is the way to make an individual octopus:

1. Wrap yarn 24 times around a 5 inch square of cardboard in one direction, or around the fingers of your left hand, spread to a span of about 5 inches. Making 24 complete circles of

yarn will mean 48 strands of yarn on the combined sides of the cardboard or your hand. (Remember this number for dividing later into the 8 tentacles.)

2. Tie a double strand of contrasting yarn through the head of the octopus, or the top of the cardboard, making a firm knot and bow. Again with double contrasting yarn, tie a tight circle less than a third of the way down from the bow to form the neck of the octopus. This would be about 1½ inches from the place where you've secured the knot for the top of the head. Make several turns of the yarn around the neck to give firmness and fasten in the front of the head with a knot and small bow which will eventually serve as a necktie.

3. Try to make the long loops of yarn as straight as possible and then cut carefully along the bottom of the combined loops, so that you now have 48 strands of straight yarn hanging from the neck.

4. Take 6 strands of yarn at one time for each of the 8 tentacles of the octopus. Divide these into 3 sections with 2 strands in each section. Braid the sections into a tentacle. When you have braided as close to the end as possible, tie the ends with a piece of contrasting yarn doubled. Finish with a neat bow or knot. Trim ends of tentacle and go on to braid the other 7.

5. The front of the octopus ought to be where the necktie is, so above the bow, sew on the 2 buttons for eyes. An elementary art instructor once told me that people have the greatest trouble drawing faces because they put the eyes too close together, so even though he isn't a person, put the

buttons as far apart as possible without going around his face to the side or back of his head!
6. Trim all the ends. Be delighted with your handiwork and go on to make another dozen or so.

FOOD:

Pistachio   and/or   Banana Ice cream
Octopus Cake
Salted Nuts
Hot Chocolate

Those two odd flavors are merely suggestions to let you think of something a little unusual. We don't suggest Octopus ice cream with squid sauce, but more than occasionally one tends to get in a rut with vanilla, chocolate and strawberry. Perhaps your guests would prefer butterscotch or peach. When you serve a fairly novel flavor, be sure to offer a choice, and for youngsters, keep a supply of vanilla in the back of the freezer.

Let your guests know, however, that you do have imagination by offering a flavor surprise. Pumpkin anyone?

Make a chocolate or yellow cake and top it with fluffy white frosting. In the center place a large black gumdrop with eight tentacles of black licorice sticks. Yes, you could use a red gumdrop and red stick candy, if you prefer.

Hot chocolate makes a good winter beverage. For warmer months, you may want to substitute ginger ale or cream soda.

2 High School Corridors

Autograph Party

Peanutty Party

Marshmallows Gone Wild

Mod Welcome Home Party

Autograph Party

Since co-eds notoriously drool over pictures and autographs of their favorite movie stars, band leaders, and singing groups, a teen-age autograph party seems like a natural vehicle for a high school girl to suggest—and one did.

An autograph party to adults and particularly to authors involves the selling of books with the person who wrote them adding his or her own name in the mood and spirit of good business publicity.

Not so, however, with this party—you needn't be a celebrity nor even an author; you needn't have sung on TV nor have a fan club named after you; you needn't have cut a record nor even be able to carry a tune. This is an Autograph Party for YOU, for everybody, for anyone who can write his name!

INVITATIONS: Write your invitations on scraps of old material and specify the time, date and place of the party. Underline emphatically that each guest should wear an *old shirt*.

DECORATIONS: Mount pictures of all kinds of people on construction paper frames. Add to these the photos of some of your teachers and friends. Get as many as possible autographed for the occasion.

Letters, humorous, or otherwise, might also be similarly framed and mounted on the wall, with the "autograph" of the writer encircled in red ink.

Book jackets with author's name enlarged to go with the motif

47

would add some interest. Lots of blank checks made out for one million dollars, waiting for the "autograph" would also tease your guests' fancies.

AUTOGRAPH MATCHING

FUN: Cut out twelve pictures of famous people and mount them on poster board, but put the wrong name under each. Give all guests pencils and paper and have them make their own list of photographs with the proper names matched in correct order.

To simplify identification, assign a number to each photo. The prize for this game might be one issue of a currently popular movie magazine.

AUTOGRAPH CATCHING

Give out the party favors at this time—a ball-point or marking pen for each guest so all will be well equipped for the main event of the celebration.

The highlight of the party is the collecting of autographs on the old shirts worn by those attending. At the sound of a bell or whistle each guest begins to get as many autographs as possible on his or her shirt. They may start with the others at the party and then leave to comb the neighborhood for signatures.

At the end of a half hour everyone must be back. The person with the most autographs on his shirt receives an "autograph hound"—a stuffed animal for even more John Hancocks!

An autograph book might be a prize for the person having the most difficult time securing a certain signature; and perhaps some other gift for the most unusual experience anyone had while on the autograph hunt.

SIGNATURE SEARCHING

Everyone writes the following sentence on a 5″ x 8″ card but no one signs his name: "This is my signature."

Cards are then shaken up in a box and pulled out one by one as guests try to identify the handwriting and the writer.

This is also an excellent time for someone to give a demonstration of handwriting analysis. Perhaps a favorite teacher or parent would "bone up" on the subject ahead of time, so that some wild guesses, at least, could be made as to the temperament, personality, and pleasures of the writer. Your public library will undoubtedly have at least one book on the subject. Perhaps, after this light introduction, one of your guests will actually become an expert!

FAVORS: The ball-point pens, as mentioned earlier, or an indelible pen—ask at your stationery or drug store as to the least expensive but most satisfactory type for writing on fabric.

FOOD: Authors scratch their heads and scour through old recipe books to hunt for unusual party desserts to suggest to readers. Since these parties are those authentically concocted by teenagers, they think singly and universally: their suggestion is for:

Sandwiches or Pizza

Soda Pop   Potato chips

Cookies

During refreshments offer additional prizes to those who have the most dotted "i"s or crossed "t"s on their shirts from the Autograph Hunt. Make up as many letters or letters combinations as you have prizes. Who had the most "Mc" 's, or the most "J's" or the longest name, or the shortest, or the least legible?

Peanutty Party

This is a high school party, but it could be used for a junior high celebration or an adult wing-ding just as easily. Peanuts make a good theme for any sort of whacky or "nutty" doings, so make the party to suit your wildest fancy.

INVITATIONS: Here's a choice!

1. Make invitations of construction paper cut in the shape of peanuts.
2. Type a "nutty" note invitation and tie it to a peanut shell.
3. Carefully, but very carefully, take peanuts out of the shell and insert small invitation printed on narrow paper, rolled up, into the empty shell. Glue or fasten the shell back together with transparent tape.

   Make sure those who receive the nuts, know to open them!

DECORATIONS: For the refreshment table, make a large papier-mâché elephant and letter a sign for his blanket, saying, "COME JOIN ME FOR A SNACK!"

Peanut butter jars will make appropriate decorations and, of course, lots and lots of peanuts in the shell.

Take a fairly large basket and stuff it with paper, but cover the paper with a layer of peanuts to give the effect of displaying a whole "barrel of nuts." Better not let too many people nibble too soon, or the secret of the stuffing will soon be revealed!

PEANUT-EATING CONTEST

FUN: Have a championship contest among six of the heartiest volunteers. Give each person a bag of peanuts and within three to five minutes (you decide on the time according to how many peanuts you want to use for the game) see who can shell and eat the most peanuts.

You can vary this by counting out thirty peanuts in front of each contestant. The person shelling and eating the pile first receives a peanut candy bar as a prize.

In the middle of all this eating, a forfeit could be added for any shell left with a peanut in it. The forfeit might be "last one in the refreshment line."

PICKING PEANUTS

Pass a basket of peanuts among the guests and tell each person to take one peanut (in the shell, of course). No clue as to whether it should be a large shell, small shell, or what, but when all have picked a peanut and shelled it, announce these awards:

1 jar of peanut butter for the smallest peanut
1 peanut for the largest peanut
1 peanut butter sandwich for the guest finding the most peanuts in his shell.

BALANCED PEANUTS

Make a torture track or obstacle course for two teams. You might have a table to crawl under or several chairs to "snake walk" in between and around. When this has been prepared, give the leader of each team a knife and a peanut to balance upon it.

Each one must complete the obstacle course without losing the peanut. If the nut drops, the trip must be started again.

Two identical obstacle courses will speed up the game; otherwise the two competing team members might bump into one another and vie for first place under the table!

Winning team members each receive elephant posters (even if you have to make the posters yourself) advertising this very "Peanutty Party."

PEANUT GUESSING

Sometime during the evening let each guest guess how many peanuts were used in the decorations and games. The only difficulty with this event, is that YOU have to know the answer and count them before you begin.

Let everyone drop his guess into a ballot box, containing his name or initials. You'll be surprised at the guesses—so will the person with the most nearly correct conjecture.

If you don't want to count *all* the peanuts, just ask guests to imagine how many are in the barrel that *you* but not they know is stuffed with paper. Amazing what people guess, isn't it?

FAVORS: Here's another choice:

1. Name tags in the shape of peanuts.
2. Name tags in the shape of an elephant with a peanut attached.
3. Name pins made from a peanut shell with names printed on with colored marking pens or glued on with alphabet macaroni. Glue safety pins to the back and shellac the whole peanut if for a more finished take-home souvenir.

FOOD:

Small peanut butter and jelly sandwiches
Peanut cookies   Hot chocolate
A bowl of peanuts
(for those who aren't already tired
of the whole nutty
idea)

Marshmallows Gone Wild!

Plan a party with a marshmallow theme. Marshmallows are relatively inexpensive and certainly available anywhere in the United States. They offer a jumping-off-place for a party in which you can go in any direction according to your mood, the season or the weather.

The winter would lend itself ideally to marshmallow snowmen as well as larger cotton snowmen that look like marshmallows.

The summer, however, though offering an entirely different setting, is ideal for a weiner roast and marshmallow toast.

For spring there could be marshmallow rabbits or flowers and for fall you can easily make orange marshmallow pumpkins.

INVITATIONS: Wrap a marshmallow in clear plastic wrap with a small ribbon to gather the edges of the wrap together. Attach a tag to the ribbon with the following message:

> Marshmallows have gone wild!
> Come and see how,
> when and where.
> Saturday, 8 P.M.
> at Susan's.

DECORATIONS: Well, you can't decorate a campfire in the woods or even a barbeque grill in the backyard very easily; but if it's snowy and you're in the den, you could hang marshmallows by strings from the ceiling at various lengths to resemble, possibly, snowflakes.

You might have one large chain of pastel marshmallows hanging over the refreshment table.

FUN: Here is a whole assortment of marshmallow games. You can undoubtedly think of at least a dozen more by giving your own favorite party game a marshmallow twist!

MARSHMALLOW RELAY

Casually pass a bowl of pastel marshmallows and invite each guest to take one. Then, line all the green marshmallows into one team, the yellows into another and so forth. Juggle people around to even up the teams at the end, if it is necessary. (Offer an extra marshmallow for the inconvenience of changing teams.)

This is the oldie of carrying something on a spoon to the opposite end of the room; you've probably done it at least twenty times before with everything from a potato to an egg. This time it's with a marshmallow.

The first member of each team places a spoon handle in his mouth and a marshmallow is inserted in the bowl. He must run to the opposite goal post and return before giving the next member in line the same marshmallow but with the hostess providing clean spoons for each player!

This should be done at least three times: first with a tablespoon, then with a teaspoon and finally with a very small baby or plastic spoon.

Another more devious angle to play on the guests is to have four miniature marshmallows instead of one large one in the spoon. *Increase* the marshmallows, if possible, as you *decrease* the size of the spoon!

A bag of marshmallows for the winning team—what else?

MARSHMALLOW PARTNERS

Before the party, with toothpicks and food coloring, print symbols of any kind on marshmallows. These are to be used for choosing partners, so paint the same symbol on two marshmallows: they can be circles, ovals, triangles, x's, plus and minus signs, or even numbers if you run out of other symbols.

Pass out the marshmallows just before the game and let everyone scramble madly to find their partners: boys might take green marshmallows and girls choose yellow ones, if you've marked the symbols on different colored mallows.

Give each couple a three-yard length of *clean* string with a marshmallow in the very center of the string. At a sign to "Go", each individual in each pair puts the end of string in his mouth and without using hands tries to lick the one-and-one-half yards of string into his mouth to get the marshmallow *before* his partner.

This game is fun to watch so you might have half the guests do it first while the others observe and then the other half can relax their mouth muscles while the rest perform.

Prizes really aren't necessary—it's reward enough just to have the game finished!

MARSHMALLOW PASSING

Invite all the guests to sit in a circle and provide each one with a toothpick. Make a small hole in each side of one marshmallow and place it on one person's toothpick to pass around the circle.

The marshmallow must be passed, without the use of hands, from one toothpick to another, but the toothpick must remain in the guest's mouth. If someone drops the marshmallow, he must drop out of the game. Continue playing until only two toothpick-spearers remain.

FAVORS: Marshmallow people made with marshmallows held together with toothpicks. For winter, add red crepe paper scarves and construction paper hats. Summer people might have swim suits. Faces can be drawn with toothpicks dipped in food coloring.

FOOD: For summer or fall and in informal marshmallow roast outdoors, add weiners, buns, potato chips and root beer with the usual assortment of mustard, pickles, catsup, onions and relish all carted along to the picnic spot.

For a more formal indoor party either winter or summer, try the following marshmallow-fruit salad with assorted crackers and lemonade. Here's the salad:

1½ cups finely chopped apple
1½ cups crushed pineapple
1 cup miniature marshmallows
¾ cup finely chopped celery
⅓ cup chopped maraschino cherries
8 pear halves
8 peach halves.

Combine apple, pineapple, marshmallows, celery and cherries. Place pear and peach halves, hollow side up on bed of lettuce on large platter. Fill center of pears and peaches with fruit mixture. Serve with a fruit salad dressing in a separate bowl. Let each guest help himself to one or both filled fruits. Pass assorted crackers and lemonade.

A Mod Welcome Home Party

When those in the service, in college, or at prep or boarding school come home, try a mod welcome party to rekindle all the old friendships and maybe light a few new ones.

INVITATIONS: Select hot pink or bright orange stationery, print your invitations, using large flower petals for the details of time and place. Remind all the guests to bring a joke or short, funny poem to the celebration.

DECORATIONS: Paint a huge "Welcome Home" sign in bright phosphorescent colors to hang over the doorway. Hang large hot pink and orange flowers from the chandelier, doorknob, rafters and chairs.

Streamers of gold crepe paper will add a bright touch. If possible, gather some old snapshots of the guests, either from your own wallet or album or borrowed from theirs; collect as many as possible. Paste a picture in the center of each pink or orange flower. More reason to examine the decorations more closely!

RECORD RAMBLINGS

FUN: Play brief excerpts of records which were popular several years ago, and see who can identify the most titles and recording artists. Play at least ten different selections. Give a record to the person who identifies the most songs.

JOKELESS JOKINGS

Let each person take out the joke or funny poem he brought to the party. For those who forgot, have old magazines or joke books available from which selections can be taken.

Each person reads his humor and prizes are given for the:

Most Un-funny Joke
Story With the Least Point
Joke Most Likely to Get a Laugh

A paperback joke book would be an appropriate prize.

MOD ART

Mod Art is a term that means a thousand different things to a thousand different people. Find out what it means to your guests!

Provide chalk, poster paint, charcoal, crayons and colored pencils as well as paper of different sizes, so each person can choose his own medium to work in.

Give the same assignment to all: "Draw the most mod person you can imagine—dressed, of course, in the most mod clothes you can conceive." Allow about twenty minutes for these works of art.

A mod scarf or piece of jewelry would make an appropriate prize—with all the guests serving as judges. Provisions for secret ballots will insure that the fun continues.

FAVORS: For take-home memories, provide keychains with puzzles or dominoes attached as charms.

FOOD: Cut a watermelon, pineapple and cantaloupe into bite-size pieces. Provide lots of toothpicks, and let guests alternate cubes of fruit with grapes and fresh strawberries on their tooth-picks. Provide a bowl of powdered sugar for dipping, and all will enjoy their fruit shish ke-babs.

If you are a more energetic hostess, you can make up the fruit-sticks ahead of time and arrange them in a grapefruit or half a styrofoam ball.

Serve an assortment of fruit juices in various attractive pitchers so the guests can have a preference as to flavor. From a high school girl comes this addition to the party: "Also have an assortment of cookies, crackers, chips and dips."

Co-eds are hungry people!

3 Happening Highways

Nightmare Party

Hippies of Yesteryear Party

Sing-In Discotea

Hillbilly Hoedown

A Stew

Nightmare Party

You can put to use your wildest, weirdest party ideas. All those marvelously tempting way-out concoctions of your mind and nightmares will do beautifully for this late evening party. Late evening? Yes. Whoever heard of a nightmare while it was still light?

This is also a happening which you might schedule for the Hallowe'en season, but it's adaptable for any month of the year. Nightmares don't necessarily go along with witches, but witches could be part of any nightmare!

Black and purple make good, dreary, depressing nightmarish colors around which to shape your party theme with maybe a few lightning flashes of red and orange to scare or depress or frighten or impress your guests even more.

Perhaps you should read some monster comic books or visit a Dracula movie or sit through a horror show to put you in the mood for planning the Nightmare Party. How about a late, late Dr. Jekyll and Mr. Hyde-type movie on television for an idea starter or a nightmare brooder?

INVITATIONS: These should be way-out, depressing monstrosities that might give your guests nightmares even before they arrive. Cut folded purple construction paper in large irregular shapes—somewhat a mixture of ghost-cloud-amoeba-shaped. In the center of the monstrosity, cut a hole for a red cellophane eye and glue a small black button in the center of the eye. Ghoulish enough for a nightmare, isn't it?

63

Inside, opposite the time and place, in jagged letters, print this or your own rhyme:

> Nightmare horror,
> Nightmare drum,
> Nightmare shapings,
> Dare you come?

DECORATIONS: Let your spookiest imagination go wild.

Cover a lamp with an old purple bathrobe. Drape black curtains over your largest chair and pin white felt monster features on the back so it will leer at the guests as they enter.

Purple cheesecloth over lightbulbs gives an eerie effect. Dye the white cheesecloth in your washing machine the day before.

Cover the white linen tablecloth with black nylon net and tack red felt polka dots or elongated shapes to the net in haphazard arrangement.

Make a weird monster-man centerpiece by blowing up a balloon and then covering it with several layers of papier-mâché. You can make your own from shredded newspapers dipped in wallpaper paste; however, the hobby shop in your community has the easier, instant type which is quicker and probably more satisfactory, especially if you're a beginner at this kind of mudpie-paste making. You might want to follow the theme of your invitations with a purple nightmare centerpiece speared by a single red eye in the center of the figure.

NIGHTMARE NOTES

FUN: Don't prepare the guests for this stunt-game; merely have four people strangely garbed in consecutive order in black, red, purple and white slink into the room. When everyone has noticed them (with a few muffled shrieks and gasps) because of their odd costumes and strange behavior, let them sing a song, do a dance or just circulate in line among the party-goers.

Make their costumes as bizarre as possible—red eyes on a white sheet perhaps; purple jagged lightning stripes over the red robe, and white skulls on the black outfit. A few monster Hallowe'en masks might add to the atmosphere.

After mingling with the guests for about three minutes, the four Horrors should slink away . . . and this is where the stunt ends and the game begins.

Give out paper and pencils. Each guest is asked to answer questions about the four Nightmares he has seen. Here are some possible questions, but you can add more specific ones according to how your Horrors have been dressed.

1. Did Red scratch his head upon entering the room?
2. Did Purple have on black shoes?
3. How many rings was Black wearing?
4. How many do you think were women?
5. Who had on tennis shoes? (What *color* nightmare, that is?)
6. How many eyes on its costume did White have?
7. Did Black's skulls have noses? (Maybe one of them could have.)
8. How many minutes did the Nightmares stay in the room?
9. Which Nightmare entered first?
10. Who left last?
11. What did Red have in his left hand?
12. What color socks was Purple wearing?
13. Which one bowed three times in the middle of the room?
14. Which one was most horrifying?
15. What was Black holding when he left that he did not have when entering?

If you use these same questions, make sure that one Horror *does* wear tennis shoes, that someone does bow three times; and that Black does carry something out (perhaps a lady's bracelet or shoe) that he did not bring in.

As a prize for the most correct answers, you might give an

inexpensive dime store black horse, symbolic, of course, of a *night mare*.

NIGHTMARE MOANINGS

There are probably no more weird, eerie and monstrous tales in the world than those we dream in our worst nightmares. Here's a chance to dream up a dilly of a nightmare—with some help from magazine pictures.

Before the party, clip some night-marish pictures from magazines or comic books. Number them consecutively and pass them out helter-skelter. The guest holding the picture marked No. 1 starts the story of his nightmare based on the fiendish monster or whatever he may be holding. He stops at an exciting spot and No. 2 continues the nightmare using the picture he is holding to unfold the mystery. It will be a real nightmare before everyone is finished!

CITY, COLOR, OR COMIC

Nightmares are odd mixtures of impressions and mis-impressions that one has to sort out in his own mind. Here is a game that also calls for sorting out in one's mind the specific answers to city, color, or comic.

Players may sit in a circle with the leader or Nightmare (if you want to go along with the party theme) standing in the center. Slowly or quickly turning around the leader suddenly points at one guest and says, "City, color, or comic—COMIC." The person to whom he points must respond with the name of a comic strip or comic strip character before the leader can count quickly to ten. If the leader had called, city, or color at the end, the guest would, of course, have answered in that specific category.

No one can repeat an answer that has been used in the game before. If the player cannot call out an answer before the count of ten, he becomes "it" and questions another guest.

FAVORS: Nightmare marshmallow figures are easy to construct the day before the party. Use the large white marshmallows **with**

colored toothpicks stuck out horizontally for legs—the nightmare is sitting down.   Arms might be purple toothpicks broken in half and stuck out from the sides of the marshmallow.   Draw eerie features with toothpicks dipped in vegetable coloring.

Tinted coconut might be added for hair and stuck on with confectioner's sugar and water glaze, if you want to go to extra effort.   Black licorice horns stuck in the top of the marshmallow might also suit your mood.

FOOD:

Pink ice cream
Purple-frosted cupcakes
Pickles
(Bicarbonate of soda)
Pineapple punch

Hippies of Yesteryear Party

Probably the term *hippie* is a product of the '60's with all the connotations of the second half of the twentieth century, but back in the "salad days," back in the twenties and thirties when grandmothers were young and mothers were hardly born, there were also way-out party-goers. They weren't known as "hippies" and they were neither slovenly nor drug-addicted, but for the day, they were "way-out." You've seen them in old, old, old movie clips, or in ancient fashion magazines up-dated to the sixties. Back "then" the "Charleston" and the "Big Apple" were the dances; young men wore raccoon coats and swallowed gold-fish; the women seemed just as slim and trim even though it was before the days of the diet foods, and the dresses weren't called "mini-skirts" but they were "mini" in contrast to the previous generation.

Get some old magazines from the attic or library; resurrect that raccoon coat and see if those flapper dresses can squeeze around your hips.

It's a "Hippies of Yesteryear" party, or, you could always call it a "Flapper Flip" instead.

INVITATIONS: A gal with feathers and long beads—is she a hippie or a flapper? Call her what you will, but let her skirt unroll to produce the invitation:

> Come as a hippie,
> Come as a flapper,

Come with your beads
And your man quite dapper!
Saturday 8:30 P.M.

DECORATIONS: Take the following and do with them what you can and what you will:

Long, big, colored artificial feathers
Lots of big balloons (or don't you remember when these were the costumes?)
Old, old records for background music
Goldfish, in bowls
Crepe paper streamers—nothing is quite as flappy as floppy streamers!
Beads, beads, long beads
Several incense burners, burning the *same* incense, *please!*
An ancient gramophone
A player piano, maybe, if it's available—and you've a dozen hefty guys to move it!

FLAPPING HUNT

FUN: Let your guests pick their own partners. Give each couple a list like the following and let them start their hippie search:

1. Picture of modern hippies
2. Domino with 3 dots on it
3. Polka-dotted shoe lace (a clever guest could make one but don't tell them that!)
4. The definition of a "flapper"
5. A yellow feather
6. 1 tomato soup label
7. A recipe using yogurt
8. A calendar from the 1950's
9. Live worm
10. Last week's newspaper
11. A purple earring

12. A Christmas ornament
13. The oldest piece of sheet music you can find and *play*

A mobile or a mod mug might make fun prizes.

FLAPPER TRAPPINGS

What's your idea of how a hippie of yesteryear looked? You don't think a flapper looked like *you?* Well, let everyone choose a bead (or button, if you can't find enough different beads) from a bowl and match his bead with someone who has an identical piece. If you have the same number of fellows and girls, put beads in opposite bowls and let girls choose from one and the males from another.

Give each couple five sheets of bright colored tissue paper; (the type that has varied shades of one or two colors muted into each other is particularly attractive). The couples may also have straight pins and the choice of one or more flowers, necklaces, or bracelets from a box of assorted paraphernalia.

Set a time limit of twenty minutes during which time one person of the pair serves as designer and dresses the partner as much like a "hippie of yesteryear" as possible.

Beads might be the prize for the winner—male or female!

"CHANGE YOUR BEADS, BABY!"

Make sure everyone at the party has long dangling beads. "It" is chosen and sent from the room and at this time two of the guests exchange their necklaces. When "it" comes back, he must identify those who have changed their beads or else make another trip from the room. When this game has been played several times, three or four couples may change beads at the same time to make "it" more confused. (Better have an extra supply of beads on hand in case some of the guests forget to wear them to the party.)

FAVORS: A goldfish for each person in plastic-coated carton or plastic bag filled with water . . . yes, a real, live gold-fish. Anyone for swallowing?

FOOD:

Yogurt
Ham salad sandwiches on pumpernickel bread
Corn chips
Onion dip, horseradish dip, chive dip
Raw cucumber, turnip and carrot
slices for dipping
Chocolate-covered grasshoppers (the candy kind)
Coffee (strong)
(Try an unusual coffee blend!)

Sing-In Discotea

If you can't even translate the title of this party, you're too old for it! Without her teen-age son and daughter, however, the author frankly would have known nothing about such things. This isn't the language of the 40's or the 50's or even the early 60's, but a party isn't just a *party* today. It's a

> "happening"—or a
> "love-in"—or a
> "psych-out"—this is a
> "sing-in discotea"

Generations ago, people CAPITALIZED words to show importance, but today it's lower-case letters for "in" words and phrases.

INVITATIONS: A flappy, gaudy, tissue paper flower with a long string attached, to which is hanging a miniature black cardboard record. On the back of the record, print your message:

> It's a "sing-in discotea"—
> Bring your discs
> and your guitar
> and yourself, if necessary

DECORATIONS: Cool, subdued, dim, to give the suggestion of a cellar. (It's so much easier, if you have the happening in a

72

cellar to begin with!) Hang flowers, records, coffee-pots. Make sure you have a couple of record players available, not only in case one wears out, but to try flipping similar records simultaneously. New sounds are in. It's just a matter of finding the right kind of new sounds—loud, blaring, garish.

FUN: (This is an instantly "dated" term, but read on, anyhow.)

SING-IN

Let those who brought guitars begin the chanting. Choose a topic that everyone has some feeling about (possibly disillusionment) and let each person have a turn at "signing-in" his opinions, feelings, and reactions.

Here are a few controversial topics for a start:

love
religion
government
education
parents
the future

DISC FLIPPING

No specific suggestions here. Bring your discs and flip them on the record player (if the guitar-strumming fades out or becomes so controversial, a riot squad of parents is needed to tone down the rancor!)

The list of popular records must have changed three hundred times between the period that this is written and when you are reading it. Bring what is the favorite with your crowd.

For some laughs, resurrect the discs that were popular when your parents or grandparents were in their heyday.

PIANO PLUNKING

If a player piano is available, you have some built-in entertainment providing the rolls hold out. Even when you've exhausted them, your guests should yield at least one human piano or guitar player who might get the group singing again.

All of this is kind of risky for a really swinging party. Maybe you need some good luck to make it both singing and swinging. Good luck!

FAVORS: Who needs them, if everything is singin' and swingin' enough? (Otherwise, you'd better dream up your own.)

FOOD: Food! Food! Food! with the emphasis on food!

All the Fixings for Mammoth Hero (Sub) Sandwiches which will mean:
  small loaves of Italian bread
  pounds and pounds of assorted lunch meats
  slices and slices of cheese
  onion slices, hot peppers, oil & vinegar, mayonnaise
Barrels of Pretzels and Potato Chips
Instant Pitcher Punch

INSTANT PITCHER PUNCH

2 quarts instant iced tea
2 cups pineapple juice
2 tablespoons lime juice
½ cup sugar

Make instant iced tea following package directions. Add fruit juices and sugar. Stir to mix well. Pour into ice-filled glasses and add pineapple spears and mint sprigs. Makes 12–14 servings. Double or triple recipe to serve a crowd.

Hillbilly Hoedown

There are times when everyone hates to get dressed up in his best bib and tucker. Sometimes, it's so hot or just so tiring that you'd almost rather give up the party than get dressed up. If you're that kind of person, this kind of party is for you.

You don't have to get dressed up—you can wear your very oldest togs and your most ragged shoes and still be the hit of the party. This is a Hillbilly Hoedown with patched jeans, plaid shirts and holey straw hats the order of the day—to say nothing of bare feet or worn-out shoes.

A Hillbilly Hoedown is informal fun, but it can take the form of many possibilities. Which of these do you prefer?

Hillbilly Breakfast   Sour cream pancakes and a hike.
Noon Hoedown Picnic   Start off with a swim, perhaps.
Hillbilly Supper   Barbecued chicken and hay ride.

Plan or mix the food and fun, but keep the mood light and the costumes casual.

INVITATIONS: Cut manila paper in the shape of a bare foot. Trace your own for ease, but enlarge the big toe for a cartoon, hillbilly effect. In uneven red letters across the foot, print the following message:

Hillbilly Garb
and Hillbilly Food
and Hillbilly Fun for all!

P.S. If you feel you're not quite in shape for this Hillbilly Hoedown, here's some First Aid. (At this spot, glue on a corn plaster.)

DECORATIONS: The wilder the better!   The simpler the more authentic!

Invite a dozen neighbor children in to play for three hours—then leave the house the way they left it.   You'll have a real hillbilly effect—disheveled!

Consult the comic book shelf of your corner drug store for some Dogpatch comics, and let them give you the cue as to decor.

Some suspenders, red cotton handkerchiefs, kettles and jugs are always in order.

Tack up some cute signs indoors or out with arrows pointing to significant spots like: Dogpatch Holler, Possum Run, Leap Year Alley, and any other locations you may deem appropriate.

FUN: Instead of dividing this section into the usual types of games, this time let's explore the three types of Hillbilly Hoedowns which are possible.   Of course, you can mix them.   There's no reason why you can't have sour cream pancakes at ten o'clock at night as well as ten o'clock in the morning.   And a moonlight hike to Leap Year Point might be much more interesting than an early morning glimpse of Inspiration Ledge.

Here's a hillbilly project, however, that will be fun for any time of the day.

Possum Queen Picking

The picking of a Possum Queen can't be neglected at a genuine Hillbilly Jamboree.   No, sireeee!

It must be done in the proper manner with all kinds of appropriate signs such as:

ELECT POLLY POSSUM QUEEN
PICK PAULA FOR POSSUM CROWN
HILLBILLY HARRIET FOR HILLBILLY QUEEN

Let each man make an appropriate campaign sign for his partner with the slogan he feels will best insure her of success in the race for Possum Queen.

Since you want no hard feelings at the party, you'll have to handle the election very diplomatically. During the campaign each man should give a two-minute speech as to why his partner (or date, or wife) should definitely have the title of Possum Queen.

When all campaign speeches have been heard and applauded (loudly, of course, with appropriate stomping and hand-clapping hillbilly style) have all the queen contestants stand in a line, which, of course, will mean all the ladies at the party.

Now ask these questions slowly and in order. If a gal has to answer "No" to any question, she must sit down and be eliminated from the contest.

Here are some dandy Possum Queen picking questions: (ask each contestant a different question as you go down the line. If many gals still remain standing you'll have to repeat some questions —not to the same contestants, of course.)

1. Are your toenails painted?
2. Are you chewing gum?
3. Did you leave your dishes unwashed in the sink at home?
4. Did you kiss a man today?
5. Did you *not* set your hair last night?
6. Do you think you'd like to eat fried possum legs?

IF there is a lady still standing in the line, she is undoubtedly the best, most appropriate gal for POSSUM QUEEN. If more than one lady still remains, you'll have to think of more questions. Perhaps you may not need to use all the questions listed.

Crown the Possum Queen with an imitation possum-tail crown and shotgun scepter. Drape a potato sack around her shoulders for her ermine cape and carry her around the party area in a wheelbarrow.

Hooray for all future Possum Queens!

HILLBILLY BREAKFAST

Why not an early morning hike to some unknown spot? Just set the guests walking but have signs posted reading:

2 miles to Sour Cream Pancakes
1½ miles to Coffeepot Rock
1 mile to Sizzling Bacon
500 yards to Orange Juice Plateau

After all this hillbilly hiking, make certain you have lots of food. You'll probably need to double or triple the recipe for sour cream pancakes. Here's a menu:

Orange Juice in paper cups (good size cups, however, after that *long* hike—even if it was over city streets and unknown alleys)
Sour Cream Pancakes (see recipe below)
Butter and Syrup (lots of bottles and lots of different kinds of syrup—don't forget blueberry!)
Bacon (very hot, very crisp, very plentiful)
Coffee and Milk (*hot* coffee—*cold* milk)

SOUR CREAM PANCAKES

1 cup pancake mix
¾ cup milk
1 egg
1 tablespoon melted or liquid shortening
½ cup dairy sour cream

Place mix, milk, egg, shortening and sour cream in bowl. Stir until batter is fairly smooth. Pour batter onto hot, lightly greased griddle to make 4-inch pancakes. Turn pancakes when tops are covered with bubbles and edges look done. Makes 12 to 14 pancakes.

NOON HOEDOWN PICNIC

A noon swimming party in pool or lake or mountain stream will whet the appetites of all your hoboes. Let them swim before the picnic and choose the Possum Queen after the feast.

If you can't swim, or you can't find a suitable pool or lake, then have a tennis match or golf tournament or a just-plain-hike. Or if you're utterly and completely lazy, don't do anything at all—just invite your friends for the picnic. Let them eat and then have a longer, lazier campaign for Possum Queen.

Here's a menu for hungry swimmers or lazy campaigners:

Individual Ham Loaves (ham-balls, if you prefer)
Skillet Corn Bread (all hillbillies are supposed to like corn bread—it's part of the system)
Tossed Salad (no comment)
Deviled Eggs (a rolled anchovy on top of each one isn't very hillbilly, but it's different)
Chocolate Cake (with at least half an inch of fudge frosting)
Iced tea (or whatever you drink in whatever season you're having the picnic)

SKILLET CORN BREAD

¾ cup Quaker Enriched Corn Meal
½ cup sifted all-purpose flour
2 tablespoons sugar
2 teaspoons baking powder
½ teaspoon salt
1 egg
1 cup milk
2 tablespoons soft shortening
1 tablespoon caraway seed
1 Cheddar cheese wedge (7 x 4 inch) cut in 6 triangles

Sift together dry ingredients. Add egg, milk and shortening. Beat with rotary beater or spoon until smooth (about 1 minute). Do not overbeat. Stir in caraway seed.

Pour batter into hot, lightly greased 10-inch cast-iron skillet; cover. Place on grill over hot coals; bake about 15 minutes or until bottom is brown and top is set. To turn, place plate over top of skillet; invert skillet so corn bread is on plate, brown side up. Slip corn bread into hot skillet. Bake about 7 minutes. Remove cover; arrange cheese triangles on top of corn bread. Cover; bake about 3 more minutes or until underside is brown. Cut in wedges; serve hot.

NOTE: To bake corn bread in oven, pour batter into greased 10-inch cast-iron skillet. Bake uncovered in pre-heated hot oven (425 degrees) about 20 minutes. Arrange cheese triangles on top of corn bread. Bake about 3 minutes longer or until cheese is melted.

HILLYBILLY SUPPER

A hay ride is always fun for the young and the not-so-young (but who are at least young at heart). If you can arrange it, this would be an ideal background for a hillbilly hoedown. But if you can't, there's always moonlight swimming which is popular, leap year or not, or horseback riding, or miniature golf, or just plain singing around the campfire after the barbecue, and after the crowning of that famous Possum Queen.

You could always serve what's already been suggested for breakfast or lunch, but in case you're undecided, here's another menu:

Tomato Soup (in mugs, what else?)
Barbecued Chicken (or Sweet-Sour Spareribs, if you prefer)
Potato Salad
Crisp Relish Tray (no, the tray isn't crisp, but the carrots, celery, cucumbers and pickles should be)
Coffee and/or Iced Tea
Rhubarb Pie (maybe you'd better have a Cherry pie in the bottom of the basket; there are some men unconvincible about the glory of rhubarb in any form)

A Stew

A stew, by odd and sundry definitions, contains an odd and sundry mixture of ingredients, so if you want to have a party and can't decide exactly what to do or exactly what kind of decorations, or even what kind of a theme, why not have A STEW and you can combine anything with—well, almost anything!

Here's your chance to do things that never quite fit into any other party. If you remember a spectacular Christmas game, but never got a chance to play it during the holidays, here's a chance to use it along with perhaps a Valentine favor and of course, for refreshments—some STEW.

This party can be any size and held anywhere—inside, outside, upstairs, down in the cellar, out on the patio, at a school, a fire hall, a skating rink. Any place where you can stir up a stew!

INVITATIONS: Shaped like a pot, of course, a great big, black construction paper kettle! And the message:

Don't get in a stew . . .
>   You haven't gone to pot yet . . .
>>   Come and join the stewing fun
>>>   at ——
>>>   on ——
>>>   IT'S A STEW!

DECORATIONS: A wild combination of everything you have stored away. Get out the holly, the Easter baskets, the New

81

Year bells, the Thanksgiving turkeys. Put a goodly number of them in a stew pot in the center of the room and hang the others in odd, showy spots.

This is also the time to use up that Hallowe'en paper tablecloth you had left from last year and all those odd assortments of holiday napkins. Your friends will be in a stew just trying to figure out what month it really is!

FUN: Almost anything can go into a stew, so almost any kind of favorite recreation is appropriate. Mix and match the types. You don't want too many carrots and too few onions and the same is true with relays and paper-pencil games.

Have a STEW of fun!

True Confessions

True Confessions ought to be good for your soul and for the Stew. Put a large bowl of popcorn, gumdrops, matchsticks, buttons or dried corn on a table in the center of the room—any small item—with enough pieces so that all guests could take as many as ten articles from the bowl. You could even use pieces of a jig-saw puzzle (you know the kind that's missing six pieces but you hate to throw it away, because the boat was *so* pretty when it was all put together?)

This is a good use for the puzzle—there'll be more than six pieces missing when this game is over.

Read the following sentences aloud slowly. Those who have to answer "yes" to any question, must go to the center of the room and pick up a gumdrop, matchstick, puzzle piece or whatever is in the bowl. Each person picks another piece, each time his or her answer is "yes."

1. Have you ever read a book by J. D. Salinger?
2. Have you ever entered a sweepstakes contest?
3. Have you ever been to a horse race?
4. Have you ever passed a nudist colony and looked?
5. Have you ever worn a bikini?
6. Have you ever dated a redhead?
7. Have you ever had one of your checks bounce?

8. Have you ever gotten a traffic ticket?
9. Have you ever eaten a raw oyster?
10. Have you ever mixed salt and sugar for an April Fool trick?
11. Have you ever kept a diary?
12. Have you ever been embarrassed while you were swimming?
13. Have you ever run away from home?
14. Have you ever had the chicken pox?
15. Have you a polka dot shirt or dress in your closet now?
16. Have you ever owned a goldfish?
17. Have you kissed someone today?

Now have everyone count their pieces or gumdrops. The person who has the fewest might be given a small box of candy and the guest who has the most be awarded a lemon or a jar of pickles.

BELT WIGGLING

Here's a game to play *before* you're filled up with stew, so the belt will go around your waist and the elastic not get stuck by puffed-up you from too much stew.

This is a relay, so divide your guests into two or three teams. The first person on each team must run forward to a goal and do the following things with the equipment (man's shirt, man's leather belt, circle of heavy elastic) in this order:

1. Put on man's shirt and button all buttons, including those on cuffs.
2. Put on man's leather belt and fasten it around shirt.
3. Put heavy elastic circle over head and bring it down over body and finally step out of it.
4. Take off belt and shirt after unbuttoning all buttons including those on cuffs.
5. Deposit equipment in pile and run back to line for next person to complete the belt wiggling.

Make sure you have identical equipment for the three teams who are competing.

Members of the winning team might each receive a licorice belt (a long pliable licorice stick) as a reward.

STEW MAKING

Keep the same three teams as in the relay above, but this time let everyone join in the Stew Making. Carrots, potatoes, and onions are three of the traditional ingredients in STEW, so place one of *each* of these vegetables in front of the first person of each team.

Using only the handle of a spoon, each person must roll first the potato, then the carrot and finally the onion to a goal some twenty feet ahead and then back to place for the next person on the team to try his spoon rolling in this unusual "Stew Making."

STEW INGREDIENTS

This is a just-for-fun break in the party idea that can be used just before refreshments. Let everyone, particularly the men, write down on a piece of paper everything they would put into a stew. Pass the papers to the right in a circle. Have one person equipped with a blackboard and chalk or poster board and marker to write down every different ingredient included in the recipes.

One person begins by reading all the ingredients on the paper he or she is holding. These items would all be listed, because they would be called out for the first time. As others read the recipes on the papers they hold, only new ingredients are listed.

It should be a wild and weird recipe when all are listed. It may be surprising what some may add. What do men think is in stew, anyhow?

CARROT CAKE

2 cups sugar	1⅓ cups salad oil
3 cups flour	2 eggs, beaten
1 teaspoon soda	1 cup chopped nuts
½ teaspoon salt	1 cup crushed pineapple, drained
1 teaspoon cinnamon	1 teaspoon vanilla
2 cups carrots, coarsely grated	½ teaspoon almond flavoring
	1 teaspoon lemon juice

Combine dry ingredients in large mixing bowl. Add carrots, salad oil and eggs. Beat until well mixed. Add other ingredients and stir. Put batter in two large or three small loaf pans which have been oiled and floured. Bake at 350 degrees for one hour.

FAVOR: A Carrot—everyone can use it to carve his own figure or whittle his favorite pet. If the guests prefer, they can take them home for their own STEW.

FOOD:

STEW—Stew—stew
Hard rolls and butter
Cole Slaw   Relish tray
Carrot cake
Coffee

4   Winding Alleys

Protest Party

Last Chance Party

Do Your Own Thing Party

Scrappy Scramble

Protest Party

There are protests today for which I have deep feeling and concern, and there are protests which may irritate both you and me. Yet protests seem here to stay. Three students at a leading university advertised recently that they would protest *for* you as "Proxy Pickets" at the price of five pickets for seventeen dollars an hour!

Let's prove we don't need anyone else to protest at least our humorous and trivial viewpoints by having a PROTEST Party. It's important not to lose the ability to smile at ourselves and perhaps even laugh at our own foibles.

Maybe the laugh will be on you, but let's hope everybody will enter into the spirit of the evening and laugh at themselves. Don't you think it's worth trying to find out who *does* have a sense of humor?

INVITATIONS: Mount a small card on a toothpick and print "PROTEST" in large letters on the front, and in small letters, "party," underneath. On the opposite side of the card print jaggedly the time, place and notice to "Bring your most petty protest!"

DECORATIONS: Protest signs of all sizes, shapes, colors and lettering ought to clutter the room. A number of clever plastic dolls are available to hold signs effectively. *Do* make them humorous:

DOWN WITH SPINACH—UP WITH RUTABAGA
NO CHILI TODAY—BUT HOT TAMALES
HOUSEWIVES PROTEST VACATION DISHWASHING
NO HOMEWORK ON SEVEN-DAY WEEK-ENDS!
HOLIDAYS WITH DOUBLE PAY
AIR PUDDING—FOOD WITHOUT STAMPS OR MONEY

PROTESTING TELEGRAMS

FUN: Give each person pencil and paper and have the guests print the letters I PROTEST down the left-hand side of the page. Now give directions to write a telegram using those letters for the beginning of each word, airing your most alphabetical protest. Two possibilities might be:

I	I
Protest	Protest
Resolutely	Respectfully
Ordering	Obeying
Toothbrushes	Trivial
Every	Emissaries
Second	Sent
Thursday.	Today.

When all have been read aloud, the telegram voted the most clever might be given a frame and an aluminum foil medallion.

BALLOT BOX PROTESTS

Just in case, since the receipt of your invitation, each of your guests has spent several dozen hours dreaming up his most petty protest, produce a large ballot box (or at least a cardboard carton with a hole in the center) and invite each person to write down in sixteen words or less his most petty pet gripe. No one signs a name and gripes should be printed so handwriting cannot be recognized.

When all the protests have been collected, shake the ballot box well, and let each guest draw out and read one gripe. As each is read, the group attempts to guess who has "protested." If you can't think of anything to gripe about, here are some starters:

Ants in the house AND beetles AND MICE.
Inner plastic linings of cake mixes that have to be opened with your teeth.
My wife's new hat with the 129 feathers.
My husband's television ball games.
My daughter's short dresses.
My baby's 2 A.M. feedings.
Melty soap left in the bathtub.
Dirty dishes after a party.
Snoopy neighbors.
Stalled engines on 10 degree mornings.
Loose and lost buttons.

The prize to the biggest protester or one most difficult to guess might be a ticket to a local sauna bath so he could get reheated on his gripes!

GUITAR DRUMMINGS

Relax from your protestings for a few moments and relax as your favorite guitar player twangs out a few tunes and you join in with the music. There's nothing like protesting with rhythm and some mild and mellow songs. It's a mood-lifting interlude, so smile and relax *with* your guests.

FAVORS: Using a toothpick and food coloring, print on flat pieces of bubble gum (the pink kind that comes with baseball cards, etc.) "I protest calories!" Glue these with confectioner's sugar and water paste to a toothpick and, when dry, insert in large gumdrops.

If you're lazy (about the bubble gum and the food color printing) you can make the same signs on paper, stick them with the toothpicks and then into the assorted colored gumdrops.

FOOD: In spite of the favors protesting calories, here's an easy dessert that's loaded with fattening goodies.   Serve hot gingerbread with applesauce on top and then a generous blob of whipped cream.   Well, add a maraschino cherry, too, if you'd like.

In spite of weak protests, you may find your guests agreeing to seconds!

Last Chance Party

Some close friends of ours actually received this invitation (see below) on a piece of plain white paper in a plain envelope. It arrived, however, at the time they had been receiving a number of threatening phone calls arising out of a court case. When they read the contents of the envelope, they immediately called the F.B.I. who came and investigated. Imagine their chagrin to find out the next day that the letter was actually from a friend and was meant as an invitation to a Last Chance Party.

Maybe you had better sign your name as well as your thumbprint on your invitations!

INVITATIONS: On a white sheet of paper, print irregularly: This may be your Last Chance—you will receive a Telephone Call tomorrow. (Signed)

(An inky thumbprint *could* be the only signature, if you don't want to take warning from the paragraph above.)

DECORATIONS: Well, it all depends how gory you want to get whether or not you hang a knotted noose from the ceiling, but at least you could have:

an open ladder for everyone to walk under
a meandering black cat
a clock with hands pointed to Midnight

several Last Wills and Testaments on walls (marked with large
legal seals and ribbons)
several aces of spades laid out in conspicuous spots

If you want to make this a costume affair, you might add a
postscript to your invitations, which would then create natural
decorations: "Come dressed as your favorite criminal or in-
vestigator."

CRIMINALS, DETECTIVES AND SPIES

FUN: Give out pencils and papers with the following scrambled
criminals, detectives and spies. The first person to unscramble
the names correctly might receive a mystery-thriller paperback.

RD OTNSAW	(Dr. Watson)
LA EPOACN	(Al Capone)
SEMJA DOBN	(James Bond)
AATM IARH	(Mata Hari)
RNOE EOLFW	(Nero Wolfe)
LEGINLIRD	(Dillinger)
HOESKLCR ELSOHM	(Sherlock Holmes)

Add your own favorites to this list. It may be your Last
Chance!

THUMBPRINTS AND "WANTED" POSTERS

Before the party, secure from each guest a baby picture that
can be mounted (carefully, with photo hinges so it can be returned intact) on each individual "Wanted" poster. As people
arrive, let them push their thumbs onto an ink pad and then sign
their "Wanted" posters with thumbprints. Place the posters with
their pictures and thumbprints mounted in a long "Rogues' Gallery" on one wall of the party room. None should be marked
with names or giveaway initials, but they should have a *Wanted*
number over each picture.

The object of the game is to identify from their baby pictures the adult identity of all the *wanted* guests. Answer sheets might look like this:

6341-9789	John Martin
33221-7676	Bev Jones
11110-0001	Sam Jones Smith

A prize for the best identification of the numbers and pictures in the Rogues Gallery might be a booklet containing correct Zip Code numbers throughout the United States!

DID THE BUTLER DO IT?

This game of attempting to solve brief mystery thrillers can be played either as an individual pencil and paper game or as a team competition. If teams are used, divide your guests into four groups and, after the reading of each mystery tale, make a group decision on "Who did it?" or "How?"

Have a fairly expert, ghostly or ghoulish sounding friend read a spine-tingling mystery short-short and let the individuals or teams guess the solution. These short mysteries may be found in crossword puzzle books, or magazines, mystery monthlies, or perhaps in your local library under "Detective Short-Shorts."

Use three or four of these, if the reading of each one does not exceed five minutes.

A mystery magazine to the winner, if it is an individual, or a small box of Mystery Chocolates, if it is a team victory.

MYSTERY IN A CORNER

You know your guests better than anyone else and perhaps your friends would rather break into smaller groups for part of their Last Chance evening. Arrange several "mystery games" in various corners of the room and assign those wearing "red" to one corner; those having "stripes" on to another game, and so on until some sort of equal division has been devised.

Games you might use with mystery themes include these which are suitable for everyone, age ten through adult:

"CLUE" ® *—Parker Brothers, Inc. (* Trademark for its Detective Game Equipment)
   Complete with Detective Notes, Weapons, Rooms and such suspects as Col. Mustard, Prof. Plum, Miss Scarlett and Mrs. White

SHERLOCK HOLMES—"Murder on the Orient Express"—Ideal Toy Corporation
   The toss of the die, the turn of a card and 2–4 players compete to unravel a fiendish crime and bring a dastardly criminal to justice.

ELLERY QUEEN—"The Case of the Elusive Assassin"—Ideal Toy Corporation
   With the help of Information cards and Bonus clue cards, 2–4 players compete to track down a murderous fugitive.

FU MANCHU HIDDEN BOARD—Ideal Toy Corporation
   The insidious Dr. Fu leads 2–4 players on a circuitous chase—threatened by his stealthy hatchet men and other dangers.

FAVORS: Toy handcuffs for each guest. Just who is going to catch whom?

FOOD: Striped cake and "numbered" punch.
   Make a three-layered cake in stripes of chocolate, white, and chocolate. Frost the cake with a vanilla butter icing and then make stripes across it with melted semi-sweet chocolate.
   An easy punch can be made from mixed fruit juices with ginger-ale added at the last moment. You can plan on three quarts of fruit juices to one large bottle of ginger-ale. Don't forget to freeze some ice-rings in your gelatin molds a few days before the party, if you plan to use your punch bowl.
   Individual ice-cubes make the numbered punch. For each guest, place a plastic number in an ice cube section and freeze the cube around the number. These figures are often available in variety or dime stores as candle holders for children's birthday

cakes. If you can't find these, you can always sterilize some inexpensive plastic dice and freeze one in each cube section.

If you use the numbers, you might hide a secret number inside the cake and the person picking up the punch glass with the winning numbered ice cube might receive highly engraved "Pardon" or at least a "Last Will and Testament."

Do Your Own Thing Party

Want to have a party, but not much bother, trouble, work or nuisance? Then this is the affair for you—a party where the guests do all the work from putting together their own invitations, to hanging their own streamers, and cooking their own refreshments!

This is the era of "audience participation" shows on television, and doctors lecture on "participation sports where more people get more exercise," so why not try a "guest participation" party?

Yours is the clean-up job afterwards, however!

INVITATIONS: Write a groovy, swingy invitation on light tagboard with large and small letters using a number of different colored marking pencils. Then cut each invitation into about eight odd pieces, like a jig-saw puzzle, and put the pieces in an envelope. Mail a similar jig-saw invitation to each prospective guest.

"Do your own thing" invitations they're called!

DECORATIONS: Get lots of rolls of narrow crepe paper for streamers, balloons, bells, and what-have-you. Do nothing with them at all except pile them in corner with equipment like scissors, glue, step ladders, and thumb-tacks.

It's a "do your own thing" party, so let decorating be the first item on the fun agenda. You'll discover that your guests may have lots more clever ideas for streamer-hanging than *you* had possibly planned. Besides, think of the time, effort and stepladder collapsing this idea has saved you.

FUN: Well, when the decorating is done, the party will have officially begun, but what else can you snag your unsuspecting friends into contributing to their own fun and entertainment? Why not put them to statue-sculpting for the next event?

SUFFERING SCULPTURING!

Not enough sculpture, statuary and pseudo-works of art in your decorations? Well, here's the chance to add a good many portraits that may permanently prove that man is ultimately made of clay.

Have each guest write his name on a piece of paper. Shake the names well in a hat or bowl and let each person draw out a name other than his own. No one should reveal what name he has pulled.

Now provide each guest with a dime ball or sheet of clay and taffy-apple stick (not the taffy-apple, just the stick) for a stylus. Each person is to fashion the head of the man or woman whose name he has drawn, trying not to reveal by too close observation whom he is sculpting.

Use clay of various colors, and have small extra balls of clay of contrasting shades for guests to use in forming odd extremities like noses and ears.

Set a fifteen minute time limit for the sculpting. Prize may be a dime-store statute, another glob of clay or a mirror.

Svivon GAME (SVEE-VON)—A HEBREW GAME

For this, you'll need some make-it-yourself equipment, but plan to make it several days before the party.

You'll need a *svivon*, generally called a *dreidel* (DRAY-del). Perhaps you will buy it, or better yet, make your own.

Begin with a square top. With a crayon print plainly on small squares of paper: N G H S. These are the initial letters of the four

Hebrew words, *Nes, Gadol, Haya, Sham* meaning, "A great miracle happened there."

Paste a lettered square on each side of the top. Shellac its entire surface and let the shellac get thoroughly dry.

Directions for playing: Each player puts a bean in the center of the table, known as "the pot." The first player spins the svivon. If it falls with "G" face upward she wins all the beans in the pot. Should it fall with "H" face upward she wins only half; with "N" none and with "S" she or he puts a bean in the pot. At the end of a specific time, say 15 minutes, the child possessing the most beans, wins.

SPICED APPLE RELAY

Divide your guests into two or three teams, each one having an equal number of players.

At the opposite end of the room, place a conspicuous bowl of whole cloves.

When the signal is given to START, the first person on each team is given an apple and he then runs to the other end of the room and pushes a clove into the apple. After the clove has been secured in the fruit, each team member returns and passes the same apple to the next person in line who repeats the action. The first team to get twenty cloves in their apple wins!

The game may be made more difficult by playing music during the relay. Every time the music stops, each player must stop wherever he is and not resume till the music begins again.

An un-cloved apple for each member of the winning team would be appropriate.

So the spiced apples are not wasted, after the party insert more cloves to completely cover the fruit. Tie the apple in a fifteen-inch square of nylon net and hang it in your closet as a pomander ball. For an even spicier fragrance, roll it in powdered cinnamon and place in a plastic bag before wrapping the net around the apple.

FAVORS: If you were pleased with the cloves and apples, you might have each guest make a lemon pomander ball to take home as a favor. The fellows may balk at such frivolous doings, and, if so, you could forget the whole idea; but for the girls:

Give each one a lemon and whole cloves which she is to insert close together over the entire surface. Provide small nails with large heads if some wish to use these for the hole-poking first.

Avoid punching holes in straight lines as this will crack the lemon skin. When the entire surface of the lemon is covered, roll each one in powdered cinnamon.

Provide plastic bags for each guest, so they can set aside their fruit for a day or two as the fragrant, spicy scent develops. Then hang in a closet or place in a bureau drawer in the plastic bag tied with a lemon-yellow bow. A twelve-inch square of nylon net in a mint-green shade might also encircle the plastic bag for a more decorative effect.

FOOD: Continue the theme, by having a buffet-style do your own thing sandwich.

Have various breads:

> white
> whole wheat
> rye
> pumpernickel
> oatmeal

In at least five odd-shaped bowls, offer guests a variety of fillings. By "odd-shaped" I mean bowls that might have had some other use originally, like: a lacquered-tea-pot, a swan candy dish, or a squatting Buddha nut bowl.

Your sandwich fillings may be as common or as bizarre as you think your guests will approve:

> Baked sliced ham and/or pastrami
> Swiss cheese slices
> Thin tomato slices
> Chicken salad with chunks of pineapple
> Cream cheese mixed with grated cucumbers and minced sprigs
>   of watercress
> Crabmeat salad with toasted slivered almonds

Offer a number of garnishes like green and ripe olives, carrot curls, radishes and both sweet and sour pickles.

Your centerpiece might be an arrangement of vegetables made to look like flowers and kept refrigerated till party time. Try radish roses and turnip daisies with celery leaves and stems and carrot buds.

Scrappy Scramble

There's nothing more "scrappy" than a scrap-book, so plan a party around this theme and you'll find uses for all those odds and ends of pieces you've been storing up to throw away or use at some mystical future date.

Having each person bring an old scrapbook, of pictures, recipes, or old date souvenirs will assure lots of conversation for the evening, even if you forget all the rest of the games.

INVITATIONS: On an old scrap of paper, possibly a paper bag or a piece of stationery that's obviously laid around the desk too long, write invitations to your SCRAPPY SCRAMBLE.

Stress that each person is to bring a scrapbook, and if they are absolutely certain they don't have one, then substitute a bunch of old pictures of recipes. They could even come and make their own scrapbook at the party!

If your stationery doesn't look "scrappy" enough, let the dog walk over it a few times, lay it on the kitchen counter so some hamburger grease splashes upon it, or dog-ear a few corners with your teeth.

DECORATIONS: Put old scraps of bright material on the table as a cloth and dig out the candles you'd been saving when the power goes out. Candle scraps and mis-matched candle-holders will help to carry out the theme.

Remember those Hallowe'en, Easter, Thanksgiving and Valentine napkins you had *almost* used up? If you put them all together there will be plenty for the occasion (unless you used them all at your Stew Party!)

SCRAPBOOK JUDGING

FUN: You could use up half a dozen evenings, just reading everyone else's scrapbook, but allow some time when guests first arrive to browse in one another's books. There will be lots of exclamations over old bathing suit pictures, or recipes for shoo-fly pie, or maybe an old, old wedding gown photo.

When all have looked, but not quite to their full (you don't want anyone even to begin to get bored) have the judging of the books. Give awards to those who have:

1. The oldest single scrap
2. The most mixed-up scrapbook
3. The funniest picture
4. The biggest scrapbook
5. The most unusual contents (Who would ever have thought of putting old chewing gum wrappers or burned-out birthday candles in a scrapbook?)

SCRAPPY LETTERS

There are letters which end up in scrap-books, and letters which tell of scraps or quarrels which a family might have, but this time everyone has a chance to write a letter from scraps!

Provide everyone with scissors, paste, old magazines and a good-size scrap of paper on which the letter is to be written.

Words and letters can be cut from any place in the magazines and then pasted on in some fashion that is readable, to write a letter to whomever the guests may choose.

Each person writes his letter with whatever letters or words he can find in the magazine, pasting odd letters together to make a word and scrappy words together to make as many sentences as he wishes.

A box of stationery would be an appropriate gift for the person with the longest or most unusual letter. These scrappy letters might be collected and sent to someone who is ill and not able to attend the party, or to a mutual friend of the guests who has moved away from the community.

SCRAP-MATCHING

Cut as many scraps from construction paper in odd shapes as you expect guests. Make sure you have two identical scraps of each size, so they can be used in a partner-choosing game.

Ask each person a silly question, such as:

How long is the longest piece of spaghetti you ever ate?
Who is the most glamorous movie star you ever remember seeing on the screen?
How would you punish a parakeet that kept spilling its water?
What is your favorite color for a dunce cap?
How many runners can you have in one stocking?
How long was the longest checker game you ever witnessed?

Regardless of the answer that the guest gives to his question, praise him and inform him he has won a prize. At this point let him pick a scrap of construction paper.

When all have replied to the zany questions, and all have paper pieces, announce that each has won the prize of a "partner" which they can find by matching colored scraps. Partners can enjoy their prize scrappy refreshments together.

FAVORS: To remember this Scrappy Scramble, give each person a home-made autograph booklet in which he can collect names of the other guests present.

Make the books of several old sheets of paper about 4" x 6" with a construction paper cover. Staple the pages together and paste odd small scraps of colored material or paper on the cover. If you have an assortment of seals or stickers left over from a previous party, you might glue these on the cover or pages.

FOOD: Scraps—whatever kind of scraps you like best.

You might serve beans and/or potato salad in various small bowls on the table to give a semblance of left-overs. Assorted cold cuts, in as many different varieties as possible, might also resemble scraps.

If you prefer to use frankfurters, cut them in pieces so they give a more scrappy appearance.

Bread and rolls for sandwich making may also be widely assorted with only two pieces of each kind on a plate.

5 Foreign (and Not So Foreign) Boulevards

Pisa and Pizza

Parisian Fling

Southern Christmount Brunch

Persian Garden Party

Trip to Tipperary

Oriental Wingding

Pisa and Pizza

The Leaning Tower of Pisa should give you a decoration theme for a real Italian party that can be climaxed with a fabulous assortment of delicious pasta dishes or a single mammoth pizza. The leaning building, which has been the springboard for so many jokes and wisecracks, is, in fact, a fine bell tower 180 feet tall which took almost two hundred years to build between the twelfth and fourteenth centuries. There are eight colonnaded stories which will give you a clue in decorating *your* Leaning Tower. The original structure is more than fourteen feet out of the perpendicular, but you won't need to tilt your model so drastically.

INVITATIONS: Use five-inch squares of red-checked cotton material for covers. Fold 6″ by 3″ sheets of white paper in half to make 3″ square booklets. Insert booklet in cover and fasten with glue or thread at spine. On page one of the booklet draw a free-hand "leaning tower" with "Pisa and Pizza" above and below, and the actual party date and time inside on page three.

DECORATIONS: Red, green and white from the flags of Italy give you a good basis for a color theme. If you plan to serve refreshments at individual tables, be sure to use red-checked table-cloths (cotton or paper or plastic according to your taste and washing responsibilities).

Have your pre-teen friends help make candle holders for the table. Push a four-or five inch candle or stub from a longer

109

taper into the opening of a soft drink bottle. Light the candle, and break very small pieces or slivers of crayon into the flame. Vary the colors as you sliver up the crayolas and the wax will gradually run down the bottle in a varied blend of colors. Tilt first one way and then another to coat all sides of the bottle. This is time and crayon consuming, if you plan to do many lamps, but they will add real "pisa" atmosphere to the party.

For the serving table, you'll want to make a foot-high tower that tips precariously. It's good enough to eat later!

LEANING TOWER

8 cups Quaker Puffed Rice	Thick white confectioner's sugar frosting
½ cup butter or margarine	Red licorice whip candy
4½ cups miniature marsh-mallows	Thick green confectioner's sugar frosting
½ teaspoon almond extract	

Heat puffed rice in shallow baking pan in preheated moderate oven (350 degrees) about ten minutes. Pour into large greased bowl. Melt butter and marshmallows over low heat, stirring occasionally. Remove from heat; stir in almond extract. Pour over cereal, stirring until evenly coated.

With greased hands, shape about ¾ cup mixture to form top story of tower, 2 inches high and 2¼ inches in diameter. Shape remaining mixture to form body of tower (see illustration) 10 inches high and 3½ inches in diameter. Let set about ½ hour. Cut off a small amount of bottom of tower at a slight angle to cause tower to lean.

Secure top story to body of tower with white frosting. Use white frosting to fasten rings of licorice around top edge of top story, top edge of tower body and on tower body at 1¼ inch intervals. Place green frosting in pastry bag or tube. Pipe frosting to form arches between licorice stories. Make arches on ground level story and on top story larger than those on middle stories. Makes one centerpiece.

FOOD FOR THOUGHT

FUN: Give out paper and pencils and ask your guest to unscramble these Italian foods printed on a large poster board menu or else give out small papers on which only the scrambled words have already been printed or duplicated.

NUOIPSM	Spumoni
ALEV RICAOCECTR	Veal Cacciatore
GASAELN	Lasagne
TANELPO	Polenta
OATCIRT	Ricotta
AZIPZ	Pizza
TAEHIPSTG	Spaghetti
SIPTOANAT	Antipasto
POTUSROTCI	Prosciutto
SAVINEOHC	Anchovies
RONMITSEEN	Minestrone

CHOPSTICK SPAGHETTI

Let's mix our cultures a bit for this game and combine our favorite Americanized Italian food, spaghetti, with the chopsticks of the Orient.

Choose four jolly, hearty and hungry victims (no, you'd better call them contestants) and a partner for each one—make eight people to participate in this food race.

Grouped so everyone can see, four individuals will attempt to feed their partners gooey, drippy, tomato-sauced spaghetti using only chopsticks as feeding implements. Provide some huge bibs or aprons for all eight participants, just in case some chopsticks seem unmanageable.

The winning couple might receive an Italian cookbook, a can of anchovies or a frozen pizza.

FAVORS: For a small party, you might try to make individual "leaning towers" from the centerpiece recipe or have tiny straw individual baskets with assorted grapes for table nibbling. When the fruit is gone, your guests can still take home the baskets.

If you have a large party, omit favors or provide each person with a large paper bib that can be used to guard a tie or blouse or else be taken home as a souvenir.

FOOD: Italian food *is* fabulous and almost always loved by Americans so you're safe with just about anything from the "scrambled food list." Here are three main dishes, including a "long" and "short" pizza as far as preparation is concerned. Accompany any of them with a tossed salad and crusty bread. Fruit, piled generously on a large platter accompanied by cheese wedges, is a typical Italian dessert.

LASAGNE

8 ounces lasagne noodles (the very wide variety with ruffles at the edges)
2 tablespoons salt
1 tablespoon olive oil
1 pound ricotta cheese

8 ounces mozzarella cheese, sliced
Tomato-meat sauce (see recipe below)
½ cup grated Parmesan cheese

Cook lasagne noodles in boiling salted water for 25 minutes or until tender, stirring frequently. Drain; add oil. Arrange in shallow 2½ quart baking dish, making three layers each of cooked noodles: ricotta, mozzarella, tomato-meat sauce and grated cheese. Bake in moderate oven, 325 degrees for about 45 minutes. Note: Wide noodles can be substituted for lasagne, cottage cheese for ricotta, and Muenster cheese for mozzarella, if these Italian products are not available.

TOMATO-MEAT SAUCE

1 medium onion, minced
2 cloves garlic, minced
¼ cup olive oil
1 pound ground beef
6 ounce can tomato paste
1 bay leaf
4 teaspoons salt

⅛ teaspoon cayenne
1 teaspoon sugar
Pinch basil
1 pound, 13 ounce can tomatoes
2 cups water

Brown onion and garlic lightly in oil in saucepan. Add meat and cook until browned, stirring with fork. Add remaining ingredients and 2 cups water. Simmer, uncovered for about 1½ hours.

BAKED POLENTA

½ cup onion, diced fine
1 clove garlic, minced
1 teaspoon salt
½ cup mushrooms
3 cups tomatoes, canned
1¼ cups fine yellow corn meal

1 cup cold water
½ pound Parmesan cheese, grated
¼ cup olive oil
rosemary, oregano and sage to taste.

Combine onion, garlic, seasoning and mushrooms with olive oil and cook slowly until onions turn yellow; add tomatoes. Cover and simmer gently about 1½ hours, or until thickened, stirring occasionally. Cook yellow corn meal in cold water over direct heat for five minutes, stirring occasionally. Place in double boiler top and cook until thick. Spread ½ inch layer of mixture in a shallow baking dish, cover with ½ cup tomato mixture and a layer of cheese; repeat layers until corn meal and sauce are all used up. Sprinkle top with cheese. Bake at 325 degrees for 30 minutes. Serve with extra sauce and cheese, if desired.

Italian Pizza

Pizza Dough
½ package of cake yeast, active, dry or compressed
¼ cup warm, not hot, water (cool to lukewarm for compressed yeast)
¼ cup mashed potatoes
¼ cup potato water
¼ teaspoon sugar
1 teaspoon melted shortening
1½ cups flour

Dissolve yeast in water; stir in potatoes, potato water, sugar and melted shortening. Add 1 cup flour; mix well. Cover and set aside to rise until double in bulk about 30 minutes. Knead in remaining flour. Cover and set aside to rise until double in bulk, again about 30 minutes. Roll out dough on lightly floured pastry cloth into an oblong 10 x 15 inches. Place dough in ungreased pan. Let dough rise 30 minutes or until light. Cover with desired sauce and any topping. Bake pizza in hot oven 425 degrees for 30 minutes. Serve hot (for eight).

Sauce for Pizza Dough
No. 2 can tomatoes
1 cup tomato paste
1 onion, finely chopped
1 clove garlic, minced
4 ounce can mushrooms, chopped
1 stick celery, finely chopped
2 tablespoons finely grated Parmesan cheese
1 teaspoon salt
½ teaspoon sugar
½ teaspoon Worcestershire sauce
¼ teaspoon pepper
1 bay leaf

Mix ingredients in order given. Simmer over low heat 50 minutes or until thickened. Cool and spread over risen dough. Cover with ¼ pound Parmesan cheese cut in thin slices.

Pizza in a Hurry

Split English muffins in half. Scoop out doughy center. Brush each half with oil. Sprinkle chopped fresh tomatoes, onions in center; add dash of oregano. Top with slice of mozzarella cheese. Broil until cheese melts.

Parisian Fling

The Eiffel tower, French perfume, flowers, poodles, Left Bank artists and book stalls! If these are your images of Paris, why not re-create them for your friends? Dim lights, just a suggestion of Parisian atmosphere, perhaps some candles burning low—and a basement would make an ideal party nook.

French perfume may be on the expensive side, but you can spare some of the domestic variety from your dressing table, perhaps. Fresh flowers are superb, but the large tissue paper roses and poppies are extremely glamorous, too, if it's out of the spring or summer season.

Almost everyone's dreamed, at one time or another, of a Parisian fling! So, why not?

INVITATIONS: Very pink, very proper, very good smelling, very French—from there, you're on your own; but you could begin with *"Voulez-vous"*—("Do you want" or "do you wish," if French is the same as my long ago high school vocabulary list.)

Pink tissue paper is a possibility for the invitations, but spray it well with some oomphie perfume or sprinkle with powder sachet.

If you can draw a beret or an Eiffel tower, put your art sketching to good use. Let the invitations create a "fling" atmosphere!

DECORATIONS: Oooooh, la la!

A stuffed French poodle, but naturally, if the real thing isn't available to dress up in pink ribbons and bows.

Candles which drip multi-colored wax are on the shelves of some gift shops, or melt thin slivers of bright crayons to drip down some ordinary white stubs stuck in some odd mustard, catsup, or olive jars. (See "Pisa and Pizza for further candle instructions)

Do you have a teen-age daughter or neighbor whom you might wangle into painting a way-out or modernistic mural?

Try some background electronic music, either on records or tape recordings. This is the type of sound not made by traditional musical instruments. You might find compositions played entirely by the snapping of rubber bands. The sounds will not be the type to which you are usually accustomed, but, played on low volume, you'll be able to create an interesting touch of atmosphere.

BROKEN HEARTS À LA FRANCE

FUN: As the guests arrive, give each one a jaggedly cut half of a pink construction paper heart on which half of a French word appears. Individuals must match their hearts either by the French word or the jagged edges.

If this is a couples' party, give the left side of the heart to the men and the right side to the gals.

You might choose animals for the words and as soon as each person finds his French partner, both would make the characteristic sound of the animal on their heart. What a wolf-howling, cat-screeching, pig-grunting Parisian fling you'll have, if the neighbors don't object!

Here are some animals with their French titles:

the cat	*le chat*
the dog	*le chien*
the wolf	*le loup*
the pig	*le porc*
the duck	*le canard*
the parrot	*le perroquet*
the cow	*la vache*
the horse	*le cheval*
the lion	*le lion*

the sheep	*le mouton*
the goat	*le chèvre*
the chicken	*le poulet*

"Simon Dit"

This is the old favorite of "'Simon says" but be sure to use the French equivalent *"Simon dit"* (pronounced Seemon—dee) throughout the game. The leader says *"Simon dit,* 'scratch your nose' " and everyone is obliged to obey the instructions. The leader issues commands more quickly, *"Simon dit,* 'take off one shoe' "; *"Simon dit,* 'twirl your thumb' ", *"Simon dit,* 'Rub your elbow' " but all at once without a change in tone of voice says, "Stoop down to the floor.'

The leader stoops down, but any who follow him are out of the game, since he did not prefix the command with *"Simon dit."* The leader should have a list of actions made up on a card so he can go very rapidly interspersing *"Simon dit"* orders with those not to be obeyed. Here are some possibilities:

Pull your hair
Scratch your ear
Hit your nose
Bite your tongue
Hop on one foot
Blink your eyes
Touch your toes
Clap your knees
Cross your toes
Hold up eight fingers
Bump your elbows together
Grit your teeth

Les Fleurs de Paris

Here's a relay where you'll want as many men on one team as the other, since the object of the game is to fasten Parisian flowers on clothes or in hair as quickly as possible—so pity the bald-headed gentlemen, though most of the males may have difficulty sticking flowers in their hair.

Give twelve flowers to the leader of each team. At a French "cuckoo" sound, each one must put all twelve flowers somewhere on him: perhaps behind the ears, stuck in the hair, in a pocket, under the arms, between the knees, in a belt or waistband, or stuck in buttonholes—anywhere, as long as they are not merely held in the hands.

The be-flowered team members must then run to a certain spot and return without losing any of the flowers. If a flower drops, the person must start from the beginning again. The next team member then inserts the twelve flowers and waddles, hops or dashes back and forth.

The winning team gets *all* the flowers. No, they don't have to be real Parisian blooms—old artificial flowers will be more than adequate. Try to balance the flowers of the two teams—maybe six for each with short stems and six for each of the much bigger poppies or mums.

FAVORS: For the ladies, a wrist corsage made from three pink facial tissues will add to the Parisian mood. Fasten the tissues together loosely at the center and clip the edges to give a carnation effect.

Staple or stitch the flowers to narrow elastic for the wristband. Add a matching pink ribbon. *Voila!* The corsage!

A pink carnation boutonniere for each man may be made from two facial tissues in a similar manner, though the corners and edges may need to be shortened before clipping to make a smaller flower.

Sprinkle the corsages and boutonnieres with powder sachet or cologne.

How to Make Tissue Paper Flowers

For an aster-type flower, use brightly colored madras-type or solid color tissue paper. Cut two pieces, twenty inches by eight inches and fold in half lengthwise. Make one-eighth to one-quarter inch cuts for about fifteen inches along the folded edges. Be sure you have cut through all four thicknesses of tissue each time. Gather along the uncut edge for base of flower and fasten on wire, long toothpick, or hair-roller pin with transparent tape. This makes a rather ugly stem, so cover it with green floral tape or a narrow strip of green crepe paper cut diagonally.

A smaller flower of the same aster variety may be made by using tissue ten inches by four inches, folded double and cut to make one and three-quarter inch petals. Gather and fasten as before.

For the poppies or peonies, make two circles of tissue paper four inches in diameter and two circles six inches in diameter. Pinking shears may be used to cut these circles out, or frequent notches may be made around the edges with scissors. Pinch the circles together at the center and fasten to a stem. Separating the petals will give it life, but some efforts will produce better results than others. If it looks too frowzy, make some more, and hope that you'll improve or that at least one droopy one will look less conspicuous if you have a full bouquet. Variations in colors and sizes of circles will vary the flowers. Orange makes for interesting poppies and pink or dark rose would do well for peonies.

Very thin dowels or tapered wooden garden sticks could be used for stems as well as the previous materials. Be sure to get a few artificial bumblebees mounted on wires from the dime store to add interest among the posies. Arrange the flowers in half a styrofoam ball with the flat side fastened to the bottom of a vegetable bowl, platter or vase with florist's clay.

FOOD: French food is absolutely marvelous, but if you're going to use the original recipes, it takes time, experience and patience. I've only made one soufflé in my life and it came out quite gorgeously, but it took two hours of exacting work with undivided attention to every step, and not a person in the family even liked it. Then too, soufflés have that maddening attribute of falling flat, if not served immediately!

Napoleons have been my only other venture into French cooking and it took me *six* hours to get all those divine pastry layers baked and stacked exactly.

My recommendation is to go to the bakery and buy some cream puffs, chocolate eclairs, mary-annes or napoleons or whatever type of French pastry might be available from your Swedish or German baker.

If you're determined to go it on your own, you might try some type of fruit *beignet,* which is what we call a fritter. Apple fritters are what come immediately to my mind, and if you dress them elegantly in powdered sugar at the last minute, they will be delicious. If you want them to look as if they, too, are having a Parisian Fling, soak sugar cubes in lemon or orange extract. Arrange the soaked cubes around the edge of the platter on which the *beignets* have been piled and then light the sugar cubes. Nothing creates a more burning impression than flaming food, you know!

Southern Christmount Brunch

It was on a pleasant porch at Christmount in Black Mountain, North Carolina, that I asked some charming women, what kind of a party they would most like to give. The answer "a brunch" wasn't too surprising, since a few hours and several pounds before, I had already eaten the following *breakfast* with them:

Orange Juice
Moist and buttery scrambled eggs
Very moist and very, very buttery and delicious grits
Bacon   *and*   sausage (both, not a choice)
Sliced tomatoes
Hot, buttered toast   and/or
Flaky hot biscuits
Strawberry jam   or   apple jelly
Coffee

INVITATIONS: "You-all come"

Southern women have a way of meeting strangers and making them feel part of the family almost within seconds; within minutes, everyone is so delighted and pleased to talk and listen that one's morale fairly blossoms like their own beautiful mountain laurel and rhododendron.

"You-all come—" whether it be by telephone, letter, or postcard ought to be enough to have the recipient dash for the swiftest plane, train or surrey in the country.

Somehow, convey that unique southern hospitality with your

own invitations whether they're sent in Vermont, Arizona or North Carolina!

DECORATIONS: If possible, real flowers

Roses in bud vases

or

Peonies in bean pots

or

Rhododendron in cups

or

Water lilies in flat bowls

or

Daisies anywhere!

"Do You-All Reckon You Can Fetch It?"

FUN: Here's a casual game you can play sitting around the living room, or the brunch table, or in a more organized circle, if this is a more organized party. It involves real pantomine as the leader thinks of an object—a puppy, a snake, a bowl of soup, an ice cube, a piece of spaghetti—and walks about the room pretending to carry the object. She then "fetches" it to the next person saying, "Do you-all reckon you can fetch it?"

Each person in turn tries to figure out what the invisible object is, but the answer is not given by the leader till all have "fetched" it and until all the guests have told what article they thought they were carrying.

This can be repeated several times with the leader changing and the pantomine becoming increasingly more complicated.

Tick—Tockey

Stay in the same circle as for the previous game, or else jiggle your chairs into somewhat of an oval or circle. Have each guest carefully note the first name of the person on his right, and the last name of the person on his left.

As the game begins, the leader points to any person saying, "*Right*—Tick, Tockey, Sockey, Pockey." The guest he points to must respond with the first name of the person on his right before the final word "Pockey" is said, and if he fails to do so must change places with the leader.

The leader or new leader might then point to another guest and say "*Left*—Tick, Tockey, Sockey, Pockey" and the person must then give the *last* name of the person on his left.

Candy Quoits

Here is an indoor version of the old-time outdoor Quoits or Horseshoe Pitching, but this is a mild tossing of candy rings or Life Savers. The pins are made from toothpicks broken in half and held in place two feet apart with small mounds of clay.

The pitcher must not move his hand in front of the toothpick in pitching to the pin (or pick) two feet away. Several games may be played at the same time with each player having two candy quoits.

The game is won by the first person who makes twenty-one points. A ringer, which occurs when the pitched candy encircles the toothpick, counts three points. A hobber or leaner is a pitched quoit which rests on the pin after it is thrown and counts two points for the person pitching.

Each player throws his two quoits in succession with the winner of the first game having the right to be first in the succeeding game.

FAVORS: Let your guests make their own take-home favors: seed pictures which have become so popular at craft shops, playgrounds, camp programs and art classes in the last several years.

Secure seeds from an art supplier or grain dealer, if you live in a rural area. Choose large seeds like those from sunflowers, or use dried corn or any variety of dried beans from the super market such as navy and kidney beans which will give contrast.

If your guests are already seated at card tables for the "brunch," it will be easy for them to work in groups of four. Give each person a 5″ x 8″ piece of sturdy poster board and one bottle of white liquid glue per table as well as several cups of assorted seeds, beans or corn.

Several pictures may be made up ahead of time for demonstration—perhaps one of a flower, another of a person's head or foot or hand, or still another of a scene or still life.

Allow thirty minutes for the completion of the picture and then have a judging as to the most "attractive," most "unusual" and "brightest" or "most complicated."

Each one has a take-home masterpiece, however!

FOOD: Several other women contributed, but Mrs. Ginny Mc-Glosson of Charlotte, North Carolina came forth with the food suggestions for this "Southern Brunch." Ginny works for a catering service, so I believe this is authentic:

> Melon balls served in scooped out pineapple shells
> Omelette—with green pepper and sharp cheddar cheese
> Sausage Rolls
> Sour Cream Corn Bread
>   or   Mayonnaise Muffins
>   or   Danish Rolls
> Pots and pots of coffee

The Sour Cream Corn Bread they tell me is a real favorite of theirs and has no real recipe except to mix up a package of cornbread mix, then top it with a mixture of sautéed onion, sour cream and grated sharp cheese. Bake at 400 degrees according to package directions, usually about twenty minutes.

The Mayonnaise Muffins are really biscuits, but are made with self-rising flour which I had forgotten is used so widely in the south. If you don't have any on hand, you'll have to add baking powder.

Mayonnaise Muffins

2 cups self-rising flour
(or all-purpose flour
and 3 tsp. baking
powder)
¾ cup milk
¼ cup mayonnaise

Mix and bake as for your usual biscuit recipe. Mine says 450 degrees for 12 to 15 minutes.

Sausage Rolls

1 package pie crust mix (for 2-crust pie)
1 pound well-seasoned sausage, crumbled and browned

Roll out pie crust in rectangle. Spread browned, drained sausage on it and roll up like jelly roll. Chill in refrigerator. Slice ½ inch thick and place pieces on cookie sheet. Bake at 400 degrees about ten minutes till nicely browned.

Persian Garden Party

Just as the very name of the country of Persia has become Iran, so the customs, the costumes and the economic life of the people have changed greatly in the last two decades.

A party, though, is not realism, but make-believe, in the very most joyous meaning of the term. Whether your Persian party is indoors or out, add much of the mystery of the Middle East to create a mood of mystery, beauty and intrigue for your guests.

INVITATIONS: Write notes on very thin parchment-like paper to give the feeling of a delicate mood and party. A very, very tiny flower might be fastened to the invitation.

DECORATIONS:

Among Middle Eastern gardens those in Iran are justly famous. The Iranian wants above all else: coolness, greenness, and the refreshing sound of trickling water, preferably completely enclosed by a high wall. Iranian or Persian gardens are laid out geometrically and feature such subtle color combinations that they inspire the patterns for Persian rugs that are prized the world over. The gardens in Iran are divided into four quarters by canals called *jubes*. In the morning and in the evening, water is let into the canals to flood the gardens. Iranian garden layouts are almost always the same, although sometimes there is a pigeon tower. There usually are narrow canals, straight paths, a small pool and a summer house. Iranian gardens are small and neat. Most have a few poplar trees, possibly some cypress and Asiatic plane. Sometimes ropes are hung between trees for children's swings. There are always more trees than there are flowers, and there is seldom a formal flower bed. The flowers are dotted about on the ground beneath the trees.

Popular flowers are roses, carnations, petunias, stocks, zinnias, violets, hyacinths, jasmine. Persian roses have been written about by many poets. Sometimes rose petals are sprinkled on the garden pool when a party is to be given. Roses are used to decorate candlesticks. A gift of flowers is much appreciated.

A recreation hall [as well as your own lawn] could be decorated to resemble an Iranian garden. Use your imagination and you will not need to buy much except crepe paper. You might use a series of cardboard boxes of the same size to divide the room into four equal parts. Line the boxes with light blue or aquamarine paper. Now you have your canals. Sprinkle artificial grass on the floor between the canals [or borrow the rolled-up kind from funeral home or florist]. From large branches construct a summer house and suggest a few trees. The walls of the room can represent the walls of the garden and the doorways may be disguised to suggest garden gates. Sprinkle rose petals in the canals. Borrow all the potted plants you can and place them strategically around artificial flowers. You might make or purchase some. Long strips of gray cardboard tacked onto the floor could provide the garden paths. Even a very simple suggestion of this neat, geometric garden can induce an "Evening In the Middle East" mood in your guests. Try it and see. As guests arrive, allow time for them to stroll in the garden in true Iranian fashion. (From *Fun and Festival from the Middle East* by Jean Rowland)

PERSIAN MOMENTS

FUN: It's rather debatable whether or not a minute would seem longer or shorter in a Persian garden or an American city, but why

not try it and see? Give six guests each a silk scarf. When the
leader gives the signal, each guest will begin to count silently the
length of a minute. When a player feels that the minute is over,
he or she will drop the silk scarf. The leader must be careful not
to give any hint as the minute draws to a close. The winner is
the guest who dropped the scarf at the second most near the
minute mark.

A small artificial corsage or boutonnier would be an appropriate
flowery Persian prize.

SHADOW PLAYS

The shadow play is one of the oldest forms of entertainment. It is still extremely popular in the Middle East.

Use puppets to present the shadow play. Because they are
flat, they are easy and fun to make. In the Middle East
they are made of pieces of leather. You can use cardboard.
Make the figures 12 inches to 18 inches high, just as they
are in the Middle East. Draw in outline the figures you
need for your story, including anything—skirts, pants, hats,
wings—that will add to the effect of the silhouette. Then
cut figures apart at various joints of the body, punch a hole
in each piece, and rejoin with paper fasteners. The holes
should be large enough to allow the pieces to move easily.
Use thin sticks, like medical swabs, attached by transparent
tape or staples to move the figures. To simulate a stage,
hang or stretch a sheet from the ceiling or in a doorway.
Back of it place a strong light with a reflector. Between the
light and the cloth place cutouts to suggest scenery and move
the figures according to the action desired. Real actors may
take the place of cardboard figures, of course. As the shadow
play unfolds, appropriate dialogue is spoken, often to the
accompaniment of "mood music" by one or two musicians.

Sometimes shadow plays are called *Karagoz* plays for
Karagoz, a rogue, who is a character in many of them in the

Middle East. Sometimes shadow play performers in the Middle East present a folk tale. Just as often, they improvise a play satirizing current news and gossip. (From *Fun and Festival from the Middle East*)

FOOD: Middle Eastern hospitality is world famous, and part of that hospitality consists of offering a guest something to eat or drink almost as soon as he has entered the house or the tent. In many parts of the Middle East, this will be coffee, which is more than a mere beverage drunk with meals. It is a social institution! Considered the traditional cup of welcome, it is served to all visitors at all hours of the day. In every household it seems that coffee either has just been made or is about to be prepared. It would be unheard of for a visitor to leave without having at least one cup. On a visit to the bazaar you may have coffee pressed upon you by the merchant whose wares you are examining. Even though language difference may be a barrier between you, sharing coffee results in friendly smiles and some degree of mutual understanding.

It is not surprising that there are many traditions and superstitions about coffee. In Iran a guest should always accept his cup from the host in his right hand; to take it with the left is considered impolite. A favorite pastime at many parties is for everyone to invert his cup and let the sediment (in properly prepared Turkish coffee there is always sediment in the bottom of the cup) cool and run, making designs on the side of the cup. Then one of the guests will read the future of each person present. At this party, you may have one person pretend to be a "coffee reader." Pick someone with plenty of imagination and who talks easily. (From *Fun and Festival from the Middle East*)

If this is a dinner party in Persia, you may want to serve your guests:

Shish ke-babs
Squash Casserole
Tossed green salad   Hard rolls
Coffee
Large tray of cookies, nuts and raisins

SQUASH CASSEROLE

7 tablespoons butter, melted
7 tablespoons flour
2 cups milk
2 eggs, beaten
2 cups cooked squash, mashed
    (yellow or crooked neck
    squash)
½ pound cheese, grated
Salt and pepper to taste
bread crumbs

Blend butter and flour in double boiler. Add milk; heat thoroughly. Stir in remaining ingredients except crumbs. Cook one hour. Line casserole with crumbs; pour in squash mixture. Cover with crumbs. Bake at 325 degrees until browned. Makes 8 servings.

Trip to Tipperary

It may be a long way to Tipperary, as the song by that name would suggest, but by the time this party is over, it may seem like a long way to the refreshment table!

This is a "traveling" or "progressive" party when all the guests go from one house or one place to another with about four party stops included in the trip. All go together, including the hostesses so *all* can enjoy the fun.

If you had a very large crowd, you could adapt these suggestions and have a quarter of the guests at each party spot for a half-hour period and then shuffle each group on in rotation. This also could be used as a fund-raising party with all giving a donation at the Refreshment House (providing no one dropped out before that time)—but after folk games, relays and music, who would want to drop out without punch and cake?

The suggestions listed, however, assume an average-sized party of one to two dozen persons who will all "trip to Tipperary" in unison—though it may be up to you, as hostess in charge of operations, to plan for cars, a hay-rack, or an old school bus!

INVITATIONS: Send a map of your state (available from gas stations, stage departments of tourism in the state capital or perhaps from your own car glove compartments) to each guest with the following note pinned to it:

We probably won't be traveling the entire state, BUT it's a "long way to Tipperary" so come in traveling clothes and a traveling mood—we'll provide the traveling music!

Saturday, 8 P.M.

Jane Tipperary's house, 4863 Walnut Street

DECORATIONS: Travel posters, maps, souvenir postcards, pennants will all be part of your decoration scheme at each of the party spots. Be sure to mark TIPPERARY with a large star somewhere on each map on the wall with a long string leading to the star.

Make pennants from felt or colored construction paper which announce brightly TIPPERARY. If you've cut a couple basking in the sun from a Sunday supplement or a travel magazine, mount this picture and label it thus: BASK IN THE SUN AT TIPPERARY. The same idea will be true, if you can find a picture of several people enjoying some ski slopes. Cut out the picture, mount it and label it: SKI FOR FUN AT TIPPERARY. Repeat this pattern with half a dozen pictures of people on a holiday and you'll soon convey the whole idea of the party, that Tipperary is not necessarily a place at all, but anywhere where people travel a long road to fun and party enthusiasm.

FIRST PARTY SPOT

Folk Games

FUN: This ought to be a spot large enough and sturdy enough to accommodate the moving around of all the guests. Perhaps it could be a barn, a tennis court, park or ball diamond, if the weather is warm and such facilities may be secured for a private party.

Have a folk-game leader who is experienced in giving directions and guiding groups of people. Mixed-up directions for a new game befuddles the whole effort and leaves guests restless and discontented.

Here are several circle folk games, the directions for which you may find in various music books. Always make the beginning circle larger than you need, for people have a habit of moving inward as the game progresses. An easy way to get partners is to form one large single circle—boy, girl, boy, girl, etc., and then have the men drop left hands.

"Looby Loo"
"Go Round and Round the Village"
"The Jolly Miller"
"Skip to My Lou"
"Shoo Fly"
"Comin' Through the Rye"

SECOND PARTY SPOT

Take a little rest here first and drink some fruit juice and munch on some crackers as the leader or hostess for this party spot organizes your musical efforts into a Kitchen Band. Here are some instruments that might be in the culinary symphony:

Pie pan cymbals
Kettle drums with wooden spoons for drum sticks
Top-of-the-stove coffee pot containing half cup of unpopped pop-corn for shaking as a tambourine
Grater and long-handled knife to simulate violin
Colander for finger or spoon plunking, guitar-style
Odd sized pans for spoon tapping
Funnels for horns

(A tape recorder for playbacks of this unusual music would encourage the musicians)

THIRD PARTY SPOT

Here's a place to have some relays to find out who can get to Tipperary first!

RACE TO TIPPERARY

Line up the guests in three or four lines. The first person from each line competes against the first one in the other lines. Each must jump with feet together, holding a road map between their knees to the goal line, a spot marked prominently with a large sign saying, TIPPERARY.

The team whose hopper comes in first receives five points; the second arrival earns three points for his team; and the third place hopper gets one point. If there are four teams, the loser earns no points for the team.

At another signal, those second in line hop to Tipperary with the same road map between their legs.

DUMMY DRESSING

Arrange the guests in two teams. The purpose of this relay is to see which team can most quickly and thoroughly dress the doll or dress manikin at the opposite end of the room. If dolls are used they should be fairly large so that men's neckties could be used about their necks, and clothes found to fit them in some larger or lesser degree. Children's sweaters offer good possibilities for the dolls. If you can use regular department store manikins, the game would probably be more dramatic.

The first members of each team are given similar items, white shirts or blouses, for instance, with the same number of buttons. At the signal to begin, the first contestants rush to the other end of the room and must completely put on and button the shirt or blouse before returning to tap the next player in line who might be holding a pair of socks. Here are some possible clothes choices to give out:

Pair of socks, rolled inside out, which must be turned correctly before they can be placed on dummy.

Shoes, possibly high tennis shoes with lots of laces

Sweater, with at least eight buttons

Necktie, tied correctly (Try to give this to a woman—it may be more difficult for her.)

Galoshes or boots, the more complicated the better

Bonnet, to tie under chin or a scarf to be tied on model

Belt to be buckled

Gloves, all fingers in place, of course

Umbrella, raised over dummy's head

Coat, with buttons, hooks and perhaps a belt

Jewelry—pins, bracelets, necklace, tie-pin (Make this list as long as you have remaining team members.)

Each team member adds one item of clothing to the doll. Those dummies should be well dressed for the trip to Tipperary! The team wins, of course, which succeeds in dressing their creature first and most thoroughly.

JUMPING TOUR

This makes the tour to Tipperary by jump rope.

Divide guests into three teams and secure nine jumping ropes (short ones from the dime store to make jumping more difficult for the adults who attempt to accomplish it with child-size ropes): or else select pieces of clothesline cut to a more comfortable length. You know how your own guests adapt to difficulties. It ought to be a little difficult, but not so miserable as to spoil anyone's fun.

Place jumping ropes on floor in front of teams, each rope ten feet ahead of the other, which means of course, you'll need quite a long room (40 feet or more) for this relay. With three ropes in front of each team, at the blowing of the whistle the first member of each team runs to first jumping rope, picks it up and jumps three times; then runs on to second rope and jumps twice with it and replaces it on floor in same spot. At the third rope, each team member jumps once, replaces rope and returns to start second runner in line on the same tour.

If room is limited, you can vary this game by having team members bounce balls at three different spots.

FOOD

FOURTH PARTY SPOT

Lime sherbet garnished with pieces
of fresh fruit
Raw apple cake
Coffee or tea or cider

The Raw Apple Cake is baked in a tube pan the day before.
It is very moist and will cut better and seem to mellow if made
prior to the day of the party. The original recipe does not call
for frosting, but you might like a simple clear sugar glaze poured
over the top.

RAW APPLE CAKE

1½ cups cooking oil	3 cups chopped apples
3 cups sugar	1 can walnuts (1 cup chopped)
3 eggs	1 teaspoon baking soda
3 cups flour	1 teaspoon vanilla

Mix ingredients in order given.

Bake at 350 degrees for one hour and fifteen minutes in tube
pan.

Oriental Wingding

If you had an unlimited tax-free income, curiosity, and friends with the same vacation weeks, you might fly yourself *and* your friends to the Orient. You'd feast at a gaily lit floating restaurant in Hong Kong with your guests, or in Bangkok sample the curry of Thailand made with coconut milk. Perhaps in Singapore you might find a hotel offering the Indonesian specialty of *rijstafel* with twenty dishes. Stay overnight in a traditional *ryokan,* a lovely Japanese country inn. For breakfast with your guests, and with the party still continuing, you would eat rice, fish, pickled vegetables, bean paste soup and tea. (Information for this party came from Japan Air Lines booklets *JAL Gourmet Guide to the Orient* and *Culinary Arts*)

It's fun to imagine such luxury and such exotic food in the real Orient of today, but probably none of us can afford the one-hundred-course banquet in Hong Kong which lasts for three days and can cost $3,000 for twelve people!

We can't take our friends *to* the Orient, but we can re-create the atmosphere of Oriental delicacy and bring it to an American party. It takes a bit of doing, some extra effort and probably more expense than the usual back-yard weiner roast, especially since the main emphasis is on food. If you can wheedle your best friends into entertaining *with* you, the expenses might well be divided among three or four couples with each family planning one main dish.

The buffet table is the center of this party because it's primarily an eating affair. If you were in the Orient, you might call it a banquet, but this sounds a little over-done in the American

137

language, so term it a "wingding"; but remind the guests *not* to snitch a bologna sandwich before they come.

According to ancient tradition in China, the New Year is always started with a banquet. Eight dishes at least must be served for luck. Nine is considered even luckier, and a real gourmet feast includes one hundred. Don't try to match that last feast. Be glad you're just calling it a "wingding."

INVITATIONS: Look for some delicate cherry-blossom paper at your stationer's. You'll be able to find some fragile parchment-looking notes with a bamboo, tea house, or flower theme that can subtly suggest the Oriental atmosphere. Write out the invitations in your best script or if you know an expert in that ancient and almost lost art of penmanship, perhaps you can have them written for you. Keep the message brief, but make it clear that this is a dinner party and not just a pop and pretzels affair.

To a corner of the stationery glue a pair of flat tooth-picks, crossed slightly to resemble chopsticks.

DECORATIONS: Go to the variety stores in your area and see what is available *and* what you can afford. The buffet food for this party is even more important than paper decorations. What you eat, if done in true Oriental style, is extremely beautiful. Try your hand at delicate fans made from paper-thin slices of cucumber.

If it is summer-time and you can have this buffet out-of-doors, fresh flowers add the most realistic touches of all. Tikki torches or paper lanterns add atmosphere.

Low tables indoors with guests seated on the floor on pillows may seem like authentic arrangements, but if you've included older couples among your guests, it may be embarrassing, if they find it difficult or perhaps impossible to sit Oriental style for an entire meal. You don't want sore muscles to mar the soy sauce!

Give careful thought to your tableware. Encourage the use of chopsticks—maybe someone of your experienced traveling friends can give a "how-to-use" demonstration. Knives and particularly forks should be available for the timid, however.

Use your good china. No, no one wants it to get broken, and your guests would feel as badly (almost) as you if a plate were chipped, but your best porcelain carries with it the subtle significance that this is a party that you care about, a wingding that you want to be the very loveliest of your entertaining year.

Bowls of fruit on the buffet table or at other crucial spots needing color and beauty will be attractive and can be eaten as dessert following the meal.

You can't have an Oriental party without trying at least one Japanese floral arrangement. From Kikkoman International Inc.'s booklet *Japanese Way with Food and Flowers* comes this comment on the ancient art:

One cannot help being drawn irresistibly to the quiet beauty and charm of Japanese flower arrangements. This unique art called ikebana (ee keh bah nah) has a rich heritage of history, philosophy and symbolism. Buddhist priests, who used plant materials for altar decorations in the sixth century, were the first to develop the art of arranging flowers. Nobles and feudal lords further cultivated this art into more aesthetic designs, but kept it within aristocratic circles. Eventually, when flower arranging reached the ordinary people, it became an intimate part of their daily life. Today, Japanese flower masters continue their search for new and fresh ideas. Due to this never-ending progress in ikebana, the styles and schools are many.

In their reverence for nature the Japanese create a sense of space and order in floral studies. The unpretentious artistry in their designs is based on a simple interplay of light and shade, and the appealing qualities of texture, harmony and line. Behind the illusion of simplicity lies the hidden skill of the artist. Naturalistic arrangements dramatize the serenity of wooded landscapes and the cool atmosphere of water scenes, suggesting a feeling of isolation from crowded surroundings. Studies in rhythm and line evoke a sense of dramatic motion.

The following arrangement by Rachel Carr also from the Kik-koman booklet is in the Moribana style in a shallow container and would make a focal point for your Oriental party, yet be equally beautiful later in your living room.

RUSTIC SIMPLICITY

Bend five (pussy) willow stems to follow the same directional movement, with each line uneven in height. Cut the ends at a slant and insert close together in holder. Form a low triangle with five camellia branches, their blossoms in degrees of development, all looking up. Add a few leaves around the willow to conceal the holder. When dried, willow keeps indefinitely. Try other flowers with this design. Azaleas, geraniums, roses or tulips are some suggestions.

Container is a round cake baking pan sprayed brilliant red. Outside rim is covered with heavy twine, well glued and sprayed with transparent varnish.

ATLAS OF THE ORIENT

FUN: If you need people arranged for seating and you prefer not to use place cards, this is an icebreaker or people arranger game. How *do* you want people seated?

Anywhere? In groups of eight? Or six? Or would you rather mix up couples or make pairs?

Print cities of the Orient, on small slips of paper, guests may pull a scrap from a lacquered box or bowl and find either their partner or their table.

For example, if you are planning six card tables of guests, put the names of six Oriental cities, one of each four times on different slips of paper.

When all draw for their place at a card table, four should have drawn each of the following possible cities:

Shanghai
Bangkok
Hong Kong
Singapore
Tokyo
Taipei

If you have decided to make up couples for the evening with this Oriental atlas, you'll have to consult an atlas for the names of enough cities to match couples. In this case, make two slips for each city, yellow for the ladies, perhaps and green for the men, if your guests are thus equally divided.

CHINESE DICTIONARY

With nary a notion as to the translation of a Chinese dictionary or the imitation of a brushed kanji character in Japanese, your guests should be able to translate these Oriental words when they discover they are merely misarranged English letters. Print the mixed-up words on thin parchment paper and place at each guest's table spot either before or after the meal. Both have their disadvantages: before the wingding, the guests are too hungry to concentrate and afterwards, they'll be too sleepy and lethargic from all the exotic food. Play it whenever you choose, or else save the list for a surprising touch at your next April Fool's Party!

Here are the mixed-up words with their unscrambled Oriental translation:

NYE	yen
KTICPOCHSS	chopsticks
IEHRNS	shrine
OOMNIK	kimono

EMLEPT	temple
ITSFLAEV	festival
CEIR	rice
ISAYKUKI	sukiyaki
ATE	tea
MNPSAA	sampan
UKNJ	junk
OMBOAB	bamboo

FOOD: The cuisines of North and South East Asia are strongly influenced by the renowned culinary arts of China with exotic, spicy or sugary deviations notable in various countries.   Japanese food is comparatively bland with an occasional emphasis on the salty.

The basic stock of Japanese cooking is a clear soup made of konbu seaweed, dried bonito fish and water.   Soy sauce, sugar, salt, and vinegar are common seasonings.   Use of oils and fats is kept to a minimum. Delicate and fragrant seasonings are favored over strong spices.

Smallness of the food is an important characteristic of Japanese cooking.   Each item is cut into small, thin pieces.   Like the Chinese, the Japanese cooks pry the meat completely off the bones.   The cooks are wonderfully adept at cutting and shaping vegetables and fruits.

There is an infinite variety of utensils; that is, circular, square, rectangular, octagonal, oblong, deep, shallow and flat, wooden, earthen, glazed, and lacquered.   Perhaps the material of the vessel does not add to the taste of the food, but it certainly can detract. Those who are used to eating Chinese food with ivory chopsticks and Japanese food with wooden sticks can never again eat these dishes with a metal fork; the taste just isn't the same.

Even a clear Japanese consommé served in a soup plate tastes "funny" to someone used to sipping it from a lacquered bowl. There is even a difference, which may be more psychological than chemical, in taking a certain fish off smooth chinaware instead of rough earthenware.   The Japanese are unexcelled in fashioning esthetically beautiful dishes and containers.   See why you'll want to use your best china for this wingding?

If you were attending a banquet, similar to or different from the one you are now planning, in Japan, you might lift the cover from your bowl of soup to find a delicate flower floating on top. A superb fish is deftly handed from fisherman to dealer to cook so that only one side ever touches any surface before it is gently prepared, broiled, and placed before you. And your host in the restaurant may have spent ten years gathering plates in just the right color to complement the boned quail that is the specialty of the house.

In Hong Kong, if you have a large party, it's easy to charter a junk or comparable pleasure craft at the large hotels, and cruise about the bay feasting on Mongolian Hot Pot. The charge runs about fifteen dollars an hour with crew and the food is extra.

Beggar's chicken is a unique specialty of Hong Kong. The chicken is packed in lotus leaves and mud and baked for several hours. It is brought to your table where the coating is broken open, and the savory chicken is placed on your plate.

Thousand-year-old eggs are another Chinese specialty to sample. They are not really that old, of course, but are a type of pickled egg.

Ready to try some wingding Oriental foods in your own kitchen now?

Spareribs Kyoto

Spareribs, approximately 2 pounds	⅓ cup Kikkoman soy sauce
1 cup crushed pineapple	3 tablespoons sugar

Parboil spareribs 10 to 15 minutes. Remove from water and cut into serving sized pieces. Brush each side of ribs with soy sauce and place in a shallow pan. Bake, uncovered, in a slow oven (325 degrees) for 30 minutes. Combine pineapple with ⅓ cup soy sauce and sugar. Spread evenly over ribs and continue baking, uncovered for an additional 30 minutes. Garnish with pineapple chunks before serving, if desired. For the party, cut into small pieces, and double recipe, if necessary, so all can have a helping.

TUNA PILAF

2 cans tuna, regular size
1 small onion, sliced
½ cup celery, diced
1 package (10 ounces) frozen
mixed vegetables, thawed

3 cups cooked rice
3 tablespoons Kikkoman soy
sauce

Drain oil from canned tuna into large saucepan. Add onion, celery and mixed vegetables. Cook until vegetables are tender but not brown. Add rice, tuna and soy sauce. Stir gently, cooking slowly until thoroughly mixed and heated.

LAMB KABOBS

1½ pounds boned shoulder
of lamb
Salt and pepper
Powdered ginger
¼ cup Kikkoman soy sauce

2 tablespoons vinegar
½ cup salad oil
4 slices bacon, cut in one-inch
squares
1 cup pineapple chunks

Cut meat into one-inch cubes. Season with salt and pepper and a pinch of ginger. Combine soy sauce with vinegar and oil and pour over the meat. Marinate thirty minutes or longer.

Arrange lamb on skewers alternately with one-inch squares of bacon and one-inch chunks of pineapple. Broil 3 inches from heat for about 15 minutes, turning once or twice to brown evenly. Baste with marinade while cooking.

KIKKO-CREAM VEGETABLE SAUCE

3 tablespoons melted butter
3 tablespoons flour
Pepper to taste
¾ cup buttermilk

¼ cup Kikkoman soy sauce
½ cup mayonnaise
2 pounds cauliflower, cabbage
or asparagus

Melt butter in double boiler. Blend in flour and pepper. Add buttermilk and Kikkoman soy sauce and cook over hot water, stirring constantly until mixture is smooth and thickened. Blend in mayonnaise and continue cooking until hot. Pour over hot vegetables. Shake on a dash of paprika for color, and serve. May be kept hot over hot water until serving time.

KIKKO-BURGERS

1½ pounds lean, ground beef	1 egg
1½ tablespoons Kikkoman soy sauce	¼ teaspoon pepper
½ cup grated onions	¼ teaspoon powdered ginger

Mix all ingredients together in bowl. Shape into generous-sized patties. Grill, broil, or fry approximately four to six minutes to a side, depending on the degree of cooking desired.

CHINESE CHICKEN

2 cups chopped chicken *and*	2 cups diced chicken
2 cans mushroom soup	½ pound cashew nuts
½ can water	few pieces of pimento
½ can of Chinese noodles	

Mix all ingredients together and place in greased baking dish. Top with the other half-can of Chinese noodles. Bake at 325 degrees for 40 minutes.

Not even eight or nine Oriental recipes have been offered, and you'll have to start cooking the year before if you want to reach the real gourmet feast of one hundred! The recipes listed plus shrimp and an assortment of fresh fruit will make a real wing-ding. Use fruit as the dessert course, which is almost always done in Japan. It is used, not in a cake, not in a pudding, just fresh fruit. The emphasis to the very end is on the natural.

6 Holiday Avenues

Musical Note for New Year's Eve

Psychedelic Valentine Party

Wedding Charivari

Yule Log Christmas Fun

A Musical Note for New Year's Eve

The evening of December 31 is an excellent time to set the proper *tone* for the New Year. What better way to toot in the New Year than with friends gathered for a party sparked with a theme of "musical notes"?

INVITATIONS: Use white paper with black construction paper notes liberally glued across, around and inside the invitation:

Here's a note

to help you
set the tone

for the New Year!

Inside, include the vital information of time and place as well as some hint as to what is going to happen.

If you're planning a Salad Smorgasbord, now's the time to suggest that each guest or family bring one salad: gelatin, cole slaw, tossed vegetable or otherwise, concocted to bring forth low and satisfied murmurings.

DECORATIONS: If this is to be a large party, ask some friends to help you who have lots of imagination and mood-setting skill with crepe paper and streamers.

149

Arrange nut cups with G clef signs and adorn all lights and chandeliers with sixteenth notes brightened with rhinestones or glitter. Make a fascinating mural or wall display from old sheet music. This will capture lots of interest and perhaps some hummings of the old favorites around the piano.

Cover juice cans with white crepe paper and add black quarter and eighth notes for vases and centerpieces for all kinds of artificial flowers.

FUN: You'll strike a sour note, if you don't plan what's going to be sounding when. Here's a schedule to "tune up" with:

9:00 P.M.	Songs around the piano (an organ if you're luckier)
9:30 P.M.	Games of music and otherwise
10:45 P.M.	Salad Smorgasbord
11:50 P.M.	Clean up the lettuce!
11:59 P.M.	Tune up to toot in the New Year!

Songs Around the Piano

The success of this portion of your party may depend on an alert song leader (not someone to wave his arms, but at least a song-suggester, if everyone is toneless), an able pianist and you as an all-around friendly hostess to shuffle people into the door and over to the piano, *after* they leave their smorgasbord salad in the kitchen.

This year's hits may be popular with your age group, but sprinkle in some old favorites too, like "Kentucky Babe," "Home on the Range," and "I've Been Working on the Railroad." Use at least one round, and don't forget "Auld Lang Syne" now and at 11:59 as well.

Most groups will respond to a changeable and peppy song like "John Jacob Jingleheimer Schmidt" even though it may be new to a few adults. Most teen-agers will have picked up the tune in a camping experience somewhere along the scouting or summer recreation circuit.

TUNEFUL PARTNERS

Pass out construction paper notes—one t
note will have a note of the scale printed o
or *fa* or *so* or *la* or *ti*.

At a given signal, possibly the playing of some peppy background music like "Pop! Goes the Weasel!" everyone hunts for
others having the same note he or she is carrying. Some may
want to walk around singing, "fa, fa, fa-fa-fa" or "ti, ti, ti-ti-ti"
to attract their tuneful partners.

When the "do's" and "la's" have all assembled, each group is
called upon to sing a song using only its own specified note, instead
of the words (but the proper tune, please!). The other guests
see who can be the first to identify the song being presented.

MUSICAL PILLOWS

Try this adaptation of musical chairs, but use pillows on the
floor instead. Probably only the more agile may wish to participate
since, when the music stops, each person must rush to sit on a
pillow on the floor. A good game to tune up the appetite for
the Smorgasbord to come.

SCRAMBLED TUNES

Print these scrambled song titles on a blackboard or poster
board in large letters so that all can see them easily. On their
own individual papers, guests should unscramble these song titles
in the correct order:

SIDYA   (Daisy)
ENYKEA ODOLED   (Yankee Doodle)
EGLIJN LEBLS   (Jingle Bells)
ESITNL GINTH   (Silent Night)
ODL CLAKB OEJ   (Old Black Joe)
EOMH ETEWS MOHE   (Home Sweet Home)
CAMERAI   (America)

ROTN ADERB	(Shortnin' Bread)
DEI	(Dixie)
MITELECNN	(Clementine)
KEDC ETH LALH	(Deck the Hall)
EHT EEIR LAANC	(The Erie Canal)
RETEH DIBLN IEMC	(Three Blind Mice)
GDO SSBEL CAMERIA	(God Bless America)
SATP	(Taps)

FAVORS: The usual New Year's Eve horns and noisemakers will blend in well with your theme. You can assort the colors merrily to have a wild and mad splash of color. Purple, yellow, and green G clef signs on the nut cups can be cheerful carry-home favors.

FOOD: A Salad Smorgasbord is easy to assemble when each guest or family brings one dish for the buffet table. Splurge with your china plates, or save dishwashing with paper or plastic-coated ones, but don't ask your guests to bring their own table service, unless you really, really can't manage any other way. Who wants to take home a pile of soiled plates—one dish of soggy lettuce is an ample take-home favor!

Salad possibilities are limitless for the Smorgasbord. Possibly they will range from main dish types like chicken, tuna or salmon to more delicate gelatin molds, as well as tossed vegetable varieties, and some fluffy, rich, dessert-type delicacies.

Crackers, hot rolls and coffee may be served at individual tables or assembled for self-help at the end of the buffet table.

Psychedelic Valentine Party

February 14 is reason enough for a party, but given the Valentine theme a new twist this year by making it a "psychedelic" affair.

What is "psychedelic" anyway? Almost everyone has a different answer. Putting the question to some college co-eds, here are the replies they gave:

"bright colors, patterns, etc. causing a hallucinatory effect on the mind"

"mind-expanding"

"a type of drug, music or mediation that induces one to have hallucinations or enter into a state of Nirvana"

"anything in the imagination of a person's mind that includes flashy lights, bright colors, etc."

An art teacher, Mrs. Susy Fluegel who teaches in Galesburg, Illinois, had invited her pupils to make psychedelic paintings for an Educational Exhibit. She offered these ideas for psychedelic invitations and decorations.

"the subconscious mind crowding through"

"bright, clashing colors or black and white"

"curving and zigzag lines'

"not logical or rational"

"unpatterned patterns"

153

You may want to make up your own definition, ingredients or directions for psychedelic art and decorations. The field is new and wide-open. Now combine "psychedelic" with "Valentine's Day" and you've some bright, clashing, zigzag, curving hearts and flowers for a party theme.

INVITATIONS: Big, red hearts of construction paper make a typical Valentine invitation, but NOW add zigzags of pink and orange construction paper pasted across the heart.

Inside on a curved orange strip, print the news that it's really, a zany, groovy, mod Psychedelic Valentine Party at wherever and whenever you want to announce the time and place.

Psychedelic clothes might be the order of the party, unless you think your friends are oddly patterned enough anyhow without adding more confusion to your psychedelic party atmosphere. If you'd like a little more atmosphere, but don't want to cause your friends a frenzy of preparation, have each guest wear *one* "psychedelic article of clothing." It could be as simple as a belt, scarf, tie or striped turtleneck sweater.

DECORATIONS: Psychedelic murals would be fun of red, pink and orange. Invite your closest friends to help the night before the party, or let everyone splash some color on as they arrive.

Large, paper flowers are also suitable for this kind of party. Tack some pink and purple poppies to a large orange heart in the center of the room.

Zigzag some crepe paper up a wall and curve some blue and orange streamers from the chandelier to the serving table. Have some records of electronic music blaring in the background. (See Electronic Symphony later in this chapter.)

Psychedelic Words

FUN: On orange paper, with pens or pencils having red ink or lead, let each person write down as many words as possible that he can make from the letters in PSYCHEDELIC. Here are a few that you may use to check the lists by:

dice	spice	slide
his	cheesy	piece
heed	child	sled
pies	spied	heel
lips	chide	hide
pile	nice	shy

A psychedelically decorated all-day sucker might go to the guest having the longest list with the smallest lollipop available in red or orange going to the guest with the fewest words.

SHAVING CREAM ART

The object of this event is to make a psychedelic work of art on red oilcloth with push button shaving cream.

All the guests would probably be delighted to participate, but the shaving cream equipment for each one might run to quite a sum, if you have a large party.

If only a few can "paint" at a time, call for volunteers and you'll probably have only the zaniest of the party agree to a project you haven't yet explained or even given a hint about.

Provide a large red oilcloth heart to each artist—each heart should be nearly three feet high to give a dramatic effect. Painters (or perhaps we should say "shavers") should work on tile or other washable floors or on formica-topped tables.

Probably three or four can work at a time. Before the signal to begin painting some psychedelic design on the heart, inform them that only ten minutes will be given for the completion of the "pop art" creations.

If enough shaving cream remains in the cans, and other oilcloth is tucked away for easy availability, let another team of artists work on some psychedelic masterpieces.

ELECTRONIC SYMPHONY

Did you realize that electronic music is made by combining, amplifying, speeding up or slowing down various types of sound not necessarily made by the usually known musical instruments?

Electronic music has been made by magnifying the sounds from the vibrations of rubber bands, and even from playing on radiator coils!

Try to secure and play at least one record of electronic music, before your guests compose their own compositions. Have combs, bobby pins, rubber bands and a wide variety of other sound possibilities so each may choose an instrument.

Let each guest compose his own two-minute symphony, as you tape the whole proceedings on a tape recorder for play-back during refreshments. Make certain that each person announces his name *and* his instrument, before beginning to play the composition, so the pieces and their authors will be recognizable at the play-back period. Possibly you won't even want to wait for refreshments before hearing the spontaneous symphonies!

This tape would be fun to send to a sick friend, or a guest unable to make the party, or a neighbor who knew the guests but may have recently moved away from the community.

OR, maybe you can sell it to a record company!

FAVORS: Address books covered with a psychedelic print fabric. Glue the fabric to the cardboard cover of the address book.

Autograph books might be substituted with guests writing in each others' books before they leave the party. These may have some psychedelic love letters or some zigzag valentines.

FOOD: Decorate the party table with typical valentine decorations, except add some wilder colors and some tissue flowers. The menu, too, is not unusual, just touched with some zany details.

Swirly ice cream sundaes
Psychedelic Valentine Cake
Striped mints   Lemon-lime soda

The swirly ice cream sundae is made, quite naturally, from vanilla ice cream that already has strawberry topping swirled through it. Top it with fresh strawberries or frozen ones not quite defrosted. Add a blob of whipped cream or topping, if you'd like.

The Psychedelic Valentine Cake may be a cherry or pink lemonade cake from a mix but for real cheers, try this strawberry one that is a real dream of a dessert for any time of the year.

VALENTINE STRAWBERRY CAKE

1 3-ounce package strawberry gelatin	3 tablespoons flour
½ cup hot water	1 cup cooking oil
1 box white cake mix	4 eggs
	1 cup strawberries

Dissolve gelatin in hot water; cool. Combine gelatin, cake mix, flour and cooking oil. Beat 2 minutes. Add eggs and strawberries. Beat 2 minutes. Bake in three 8-inch greased and floured layer pans at 350 degrees for 20 minutes.

VALENTINE FROSTING

1 stick butter or oleomargarine
1 pound box confectioners' sugar
1 cup strawberries, drained

Soften butter. Combine ingredients; beat until creamy. If necessary, add strawberry juice to make frosting of spreading consistency. Spread between layers and over cake.

Wedding Charivari

To your "city-grown" author, the term *charivari* is a new one, even though I heard the fire sirens and excitement which brightened Main Street recently. It's also taken me three months to learn to pronounce the party (Shiv ə rē) and I hear some of the old-timers of the town somewhat stumbling on that last long E sound, too, and they've seen dozens of the affairs, so this is somewhat comforting. I was absolutely astounded even to find the word in my old college dictionary that I've toted through our homes in Pennsylvania, Kentucky and Illinois; this is the definition there; "a mock serenade of discordant noises made with pans, horns, etc., after a wedding." The etymology key tells me that it's taken from the French which may or may not help you to organize a "bang-up, pan-booming Charivari" next week.

The occasion for one such party was the marriage of one of the local funeral directors, and the *Abingdon Argus* described it thus: "John Newman and his wife, Margery, were surprised Thursday evening with a charivari planned by the Abingdon firemen."

INVITATIONS: The occasion is always a surprise for the newlyweds and is held after they return from their wedding trip. The Abingdon undertaker was informed thus according to the *Argus:*

"A fire alarm sounded at 8:00 P.M. calling all firemen, who were at their regular meeting at the fire station, to a garage owned by Mr. and Mrs. Carl Morris. The call which was planned by the firemen was the beginning of a fun-filled evening.

"Smoke caused by a smoke bomb filled the garage where the

158

unsuspecting Newman (who is a volunteer fireman) rushed in only to find a pony cart waiting for him to pull his new bride through downtown Abingdon."

DECORATIONS: What more would you want than the groom himself dressed thus and making such a decorative spectacle of himself? The story goes on:

"Dressed in a calfskin ankle length coat and horse collar, Newman pulled his wife in a pony cart down Main Street escorted by the fire trucks and several hundred people cheering them on."

FUN: The term "fun" is used loosely in connection with a charivari, since the pranks and tricks on the bridal pair can seldom be coined as pure happiness. There have undoubtedly been some which have only involved a group calling upon and serenading the newlyweds and then entering the home for refreshments BUT there are many others, too.

It is reported that one couple from the midwest were loaded into an open truck and serenaded through town. Then they were carried past a window where an open bag of flour and an electric fan had been arranged to cover the couple with the white powder.

But this was not all! They were then sprinkled with a garden hose at some opportune point. A completely "doughy" mess, they undoubtedly felt like breaded pork chops and not the least hilarious.

Such charivaris are guaranteed to *lose* friends—but quickly. After a serenade to the newlyweds, here are some games that are more fun for the bride and groom than a pasty flour and water suit!

THUMBS OUT!

Let all the women stoop behind a sheet strung or held up for the occasion. From under the sheet, each woman should stick out her hand, clenched into a fist with only her thumb sticking out. Can the groom identify his own bride's thumb?

Let him try first, and then give the other older husbands present a chance to identify their own wives by "thumbs only."

Right fists and thumbs should be used, as the left hand might be identified by wedding bands. Most women would remove a ring from their right hand for the occasion, but some wives prefer never to remove a wedding band.

Husbands not able to identify their wives' thumb correctly might be given some sort of forfeit, such as having to re-propose marriage in front of the group or singing of "I Love You Truly" on bended knee before his spouse.

"Happy The Bride"

Doctors, clergymen, psychiatrists—all spend many hours counselling couples in getting along with one another. Most agree that the husband should know the interests and concerns of his wife and vice-versa, if they are to be happy together. Here's a game for your guests to evaluate their own "marriage measurements." Make out two sets of questionnaires: the first for all the women and the second for their spouses:

Questions For The Bride
(of two weeks or twenty years)

1. If your husband were to send you flowers, what kind would you most prefer?
2. What would your husband like best for dinner tomorrow night?
3. Whom would your husband least like to receive a necktie from?
4. If you could go away tomorrow on a "second honeymoon," where would you go, if cost did not have to be considered?
5. What kind of a pet would you least like to have in the house?
6. What color would you like to paint the kitchen?
7. What is the greatest amount you would pay for a new hat?
8. What relative in your husband's family do you like best?
9. How many Christmas cards did you mail out as a family last year?
10. What gift given to you by your husband, do you value the most?

Questions For The Groom
(of three days or thirty years)

1. What kind of flowers would your wife most prefer to have you send her?
2. What would you like best for dinner tonight?
3. From whom would you least like to receive a necktie?
4. If cost did not have to be considered where would you go tomorrow for a "second" honeymoon?
5. What kind of a pet would your wife least like to have in the house?
6. What color would your wife like to paint the kitchen?
7. What is the greatest amount your wife would pay for a new hat?
8. What relative in your family does your wife like best?
9. How many Christmas cards did you mail out as a family last year?
10. What gift that you gave to her does your wife value most?

Compare husband and wife answers. Those with identical responses score five points each. Which couple has the highest score? A miniature rolling pin would be a good prize for the couple with the lowest score!

FAVORS: Since this is an informal occasion, dispense with take-home favors. This is a party given by many for one couple, rather than one person serving as hostess for many.

FOOD: The wedding cake was undoubtedly a white creation, so vary this mock post-wedding serenade by serving a burnt sugar cake with burnt sugar frosting. Hopefully, the bride won't think the "burnt" part is a takeoff on her cooking.

Ice cream is optional, according to where the party is held. If you're walking in on the bride and groom, better keep it simple and bring your own paper plates, plastic forks and coffeepot.

Yule Log Christmas Fun

In England the Yule log burns immense and bright at the Christmas season and spreads warmth and good cheer throughout the household.

The burning of the Yule log is an ancient custom when the Druids in pagan times tried to keep the sacred fires burning continuously. In the Middle Ages the log was very large, and in the midst of much celebration, it was dragged into a great hall. It had been carefully chosen for its size ahead of time and for its long-burning properties. Many times the new yule log was lighted from a piece left over from the log of the previous year.

There are few things more cheerful than a lighted fire, particularly at Christmas time and although yours need not be the size of the Yule log in the ancient English castles, the fire in the hearth symbolizes good cheer and hospitality.

If you've no fireplace, don't despair: bring in a moderate-sized log and decorate it with Christmas greenery. Who's to say you can't create your own Yule log and perhaps have it as one of the focal points for your Christmas decorations?

INVITATIONS: Christmas notepaper becomes more charming each year. See if you can't find some with a burning fire in a hearth; just put a brief note giving time and place inside. Well, perhaps "Merry Christmas" or "Happy YULE-LOGGING," as well.

DECORATIONS: The Yule Log
Add this to your own special holiday angels, tree, wreaths, bells and evergreen.

Candles, too, add atmosphere. Don't save Christmas gift candles for so many years that they become too bent and dingy to burn. If this is your one Christmas party for the year, burn the candles, even if the prettiest ones *do* get used up and are never the same again. This is a party, so entertain with your very best.

Light the logs in the fireplace, if you have one. If not, then decorate the log and light the candles and the sparkling miniature lights on tree and window decorations.

PASTY GREETINGS

FUN: Give out one old magazine to each guest, scissors and a little jar of paste to be shared among three friends. Try not to use November or December issues since these have so many Christmas words and phrases.

Give each person a long strip of shelf paper, also, and at a given signal, all cut out letters from the magazines to make as many Christmas words as possible.

Using single or combined letters from articles or advertisements, each one races to cut out and paste on the shelf paper the combination of letters or syllables to spell out the most "Christmas" words as possible in ten minutes.

Words such as log, holly, turkey, wreath, fruitcake, candy, may be included. Whole words may be cut from the magazine if they can be found, but a combination of letters may also be cut out and pasted together to make Christmas reminder words.

The person with the most words properly spelled and glued on might receive a small angel candle as a prize.

YULE LOG BURNING

Have all your guests sit in a circle, leaving a large space in the middle of the room. Have only enough chairs for those seated. You may be the Narrator for this Yule log story for the first round.

First go around the circle and whisper the name of a Christmas article to each person: wreath, candle, angel, tree, etc.

Now as you walk about the outside of the circle, or the inside, if there is enough space, begin an imaginary Christmas story, using as many Christmas items as you assigned to guests as possible.

As you mention a Christmas article, the guest having that name gets up and follows you, the Narrator.

Continue the story until most of the chairs are empty. Then quietly in the middle of your story say, "And then the Yule Log burned out." At the words *Yule Log Burned Out,* all the players, including you, the narrator, race for the chairs. The person failing to get a seat is then "it" and must start another Christmas story eventually ending with "the Yule log burned out."

Here is a possible story with which you might start. Those words in capitals may have previously been assigned to guests:

> Jane sat under the HOLLY WREATH reading the Christmas CARDS and laughing at the SANTA CLAUS with the REINDEER and ELVES bustling around the NORTH POLE. Then she smelled the Christmas COOKIES baking in the oven and she patted the FRUIT CAKE on the table and lighted a red CANDLE on the table. Her husband rushed in and kissed her under the MISTLETOE even though he had his hands full of PACKAGES and GIFTS that would eventually go into the STOCKINGS hung by the CHIMNEY. But as she stooped to plug in the LIGHTS on the CHRISTMAS TREE, the *Yule Log Burned Out.*

By this time, if you have that many guests and have used all those words, seventeen guests might be following you on a merry chase around the room! Be sure to put the phrase and *The Yule Log Burned Out* while you're near a chair, so you won't have to be narrator again!

CHRISTMAS PRESENTS

Undoubtedly part of the Christmas spirit is the gifts that are given and received. Let one of your friends in on the secret to this game so he or she may start it off by saying:

"This year for Christmas, I have received some presents. I like the boots I have received, but I don't like the shoes. I am delighted with the bubbles, but not the perfume. I think the cookies are marvelous but I dislike the cake."

The guests will be listening carefully and if someone thinks he has caught on to the idea, let him say what he likes or dislikes among his Christmas presents. If he is correct, he goes to the side of the Leader and takes turns making up more clues, till all the guests understand that the Christmas present gimmick is that the Leader likes all things spelled with a double consonant or a double vowel and dislikes all items which do not have double letters in their spellings.

Here are some more presents to make gift thinking more rapid:

Gifts to Like	Gifts to Dislike
tools	silver
doll	soldier
appliance	toaster
drill	saw
hammer	nails
scooter	wagon
hoops	skates
mittens	gloves
book	magazine
sheet	bedspread
pillow	lamp
collar	tie

FAVORS: A small Christmas ornament for each person to take home and hang on his own Christmas tree or fasten to his Yule log as a remembrance of the holiday celebration.

If you feel you have ample time, give out styrofoam balls that the guests themselves can decorate with straight pins, rhinestones and beads interlaced with ribbon and velvet for their own unique handmade Christmas tree ornament. Local novelty, dime stores and hobby shops will have holiday rhinestones and all the "fixings" if you want to allow time for your friends to make their own souvenirs.

FOOD:

Small Tea Sandwiches

Dark Fruit Cake

Hot Spiced Tea   Assorted Christmas candies

Everyone knows how hectic the holidays become with last-minute cards to write, boxes to wrap, to say nothing of decorations, prizes and games for a party like this.

The refreshments, however, are the simplest possible. You can even omit the tea sandwiches. The dark fruit cake came from a recipe that is generations old, according to the Southern lady who shared it with me. Her mother made it at least by Thanksgiving time and stored it wrapped in a cloth in an airtight container with pieces of apple cut in around it.

So you have plenty of time a month or so ahead of this party to make these refreshments. The recipe makes twelve to fourteen pounds of fruit cake, so you're certain of having plenty regardless of how your guest list expands. The giver of the recipe tells me that the ingredients make such an abundance that her mother always mixed up the cake in a pan the size of a *dishpan*. Just wanted to let you know that before you began to mix it up in your family vegetable bowl!

DARK FRUIT CAKE

1 pound butter
1 dozen eggs
1 pound brown sugar
4 cups flour
1 cup molasses
1 cup buttermilk
½ teaspoon baking soda in the buttermilk
½ teaspoon baking soda in the molasses
1 pound citron, chopped
½ pound candied orange peel, chopped
½ pound candied lemon peel, chopped
1 pound figs, chopped
1 pound dates, chopped
½ pound candied cherries, cut in pieces

½ pound candied pineapple, cut in pieces
2 boxes (15 ounces) seedless raisins
2 boxes (15 ounces) currants
½ pound black walnuts, shelled and chopped
½ pound pecans, shelled and chopped
½ pound almonds, shelled and chopped
½ pound mixed nuts, shelled and chopped
1 heaping teaspoon cinnamon
1 heaping teaspoon allspice
1 heaping teaspoon cloves
1 scant teaspoon nutmeg

Cream butter and sugar. Add eggs, molasses and flour. Use part of the flour to flour fruit and nuts, but use no more than 4 cups altogether. Add remaining ingredients, but add buttermilk last. Bake in two large or three medium-sized tube cake pans.

Bake at 325 degrees for about three hours; then test for doneness. Cover top with foil if it seems to be browning too fast. This makes 12 to 14 pounds of cake. Tie a cheesecloth around it when it is taken from the oven until it cools. Store in airtight container with pieces of apple cut around it.

HOT SPICED TEA

2 quarts water	½ stick cinnamon
12 teabags or 4 tablespoons loose tea	½ cup sugar
	¼ cup lemon juice
½ teaspoon whole cloves	½ cup orange juice

Bring water to a full, rolling boil. Pour over tea and spices. Cover and let stand for five minutes. Stir and strain. Add sugar; stir until dissolved. Add fruit juices. Reheat for serving, placing over low heat. Do not boil. Garnish with clove-studded lemon slices. Makes about 12 teacup servings.

7 Service Streets

Corny Carnival

Parties for Mental Health

Novel Nursing Home Fun

Corny Carnival

There's nothing like a carnival to raise money for your favorite church, charity, scout troop or elementary school as well as work your fingers and muscles to the bone. But think of all the new friends you make, if you don't lose your temper—not even once!

Probably most carnivals are corny by sophisticated standards, but you can play a particularly corny carnival with ears of corn as your advertising and publicity theme.

Be sure to have hot ears of corn, dripping with melted butter for sale in some concession stand somewhere on the grounds, or all your sales pitching will have a phony ring.

INVITATIONS: The more people that come to a carnival, the more money you're going to make for your favorite project.

Begin sending occasional press releases to the newspaper about one month before the actual day announcing *what* is being planned; *when* it's to happen; *where* it will be; and *why* it's being done in the first place, as well as *who* is sponsoring and taking part in the preparations.

Two weeks before the carnival, make sure that posters have been tacked up securely in local laundries, stores, banks and school corridors, with the permission, of course, of those who need to give permission. (And be sure to remove them *after* the event!)

Keep one theme on all the posters—perhaps an ear of corn announcing the corny carnival—so that the public begins to know exactly what is publicized as soon as they see this symbol and are, therefore, not confused with a Girl Scout Bake Sale or a church ice cream social.

"Lend an ear for our corny carnival" might be the slogan for one year's venture, which you're almost sure to repeat (if you've planned well and there isn't a major thunderstorm, snow, or catastrophe on that particularly planned day).

Stress that the carnival is for *all* the family—that there's something fun for every age group—and then plan it that way to make your publicity true!

DECORATIONS: Each concession or booth needs a decorating committee; depending upon the size of your organization, this decorating committee may also have to be the sales personnel and clean-up detail as well as financiers for that particular operation.

Enthusiasm and time as well as some working muscles can create interesting booths with a minimum of expense. There is a natural built-in competition to see whether the dart game or the fishpond is more cleverly decorated. But this competition adds to the attractiveness of the finished carnival so let the competition continue unchecked.

The type of booths will depend whether or not the affair is to be held in a school gymnasium, a church fellowship hall or the out-of-doors.

An outdoor summer carnival is always fun and casual and money-making BUT you do have the threat of rain ruining all your plans and decorations. Moving booths at the last moment isn't easy, even if it's only from the school yard to the school cafeteria, but plan for your own community with your own decision-making group. Summer is carnival time, usually, and summer is sunny, well *usually,* that is.

FUN: Well, all's fun at a Carnival, but everyone is bound to think that one thing is more fun than another, so the more well-organized booths you have, the more you'll cater to everyone's taste and pocketbook. Here are some booth ideas for your acceptance or rejection:

CORNY ART EXHIBIT

Corny, clever, way-out pop art by everyone from the three-year-old to the ninety-year-old displaying their talents. Charge twenty-five cents each for every entry, but try to have some clever prizes donated by local merchants. The high school group should be entering several dozen very mod entries, if it's announced loudly and strikingly in the home rooms and corridors. Prizes might be given for the most "in-significant" and the most "unmeaningful" entries.

BUSHEL O' PEANUTS

Display a bushel of peanuts prominently and let customers guess for five cents a try just how many peanuts are in the bushel. Winner gets a giant jar of peanut butter.

KANGAROO THROW

Draw a picture of a large kangaroo on a piece of oilcloth, cutting out the face in a large enough oval so a person can stick his own head in. Customers can throw wet sponges at the kangaroo for five cents a throw or three for a dime! It's even more fun, if the kangaroo displays the local scoutmaster, teacher or principal!

GYPSY PALM READING

Exotically dressed fake gypsies can make this a popular booth at twenty-five cents a fortune, with the scarfed ladies marking fortune and life lines on the inquirer's palm with a green ink-pencil. The more elaborate the fortunes told are, the more people will wish to discover mysterious prophecies about themselves. This should be a dimly lit booth draped in shawls or throw rugs with cards, tea leaves and a crystal ball all scattered about to give atmosphere to the "gypsy's den."

CAKE WALK

This cake walk might well take place in the middle of the concession booths. Charge ten or twenty cents a walk around a beautifully decorated and of course *donated* cake with the record music playing some peppy rhythms. When the music stops, the person standing on the Prize Spot wins.

Repeat the procedure with as many cakes as have been donated, but allow enough time between "walks" to allow as many people to participate as possible—twenty or thirty for each cake walk is desirable, so that the person making the cake doesn't feel her efforts have not been money-making for the carnival.

FISHPOND

Wrap up children-related items such as small puzzles, combs, crayons, coloring books, jewelry, books and games. These wrapped up in fancy paper items can be "fished-for" with dowels, string, and bent pins. This may surprisingly turn out to be your best money maker, since it assures every child of the chance to go home with *something*. Have one pond for the boys and another containing girl items.

DAFFY DARTS

Draw funny and weird faces on inflated balloons with marking pencils and then fasten the balloons against a cardboard background. Contestants may throw darts, at a price, to burst the face-balloons. A bag of popcorn makes a good prize.

WEIGHT GUESSING

A particularly muscular father might flex his biceps and scratch his forehead in the Weight-Guessing booth. If he guesses the weight within five pounds, the carnival keeps the dime donation, but if he fails, the contestant wins a penny stick of candy.

Pony Rides (only if outdoors, obviously)

Individual pony rides for twenty-five cents each or in pony-drawn carts for perhaps twenty cents per child.

FAVORS: Sell balloons in novelty shapes. Yes, everyone pays for their take-home favors at this party! Perhaps a good-natured father will fill the balloons with helium for even more fun.

FOOD: Here again, you pay for what you eat. Have a little variety of easy-to-assemble foods. Avoid the ordinary hot-dogs and hamburgers, but try instead meatball sandwiches and barbecues or coney-dogs.

Ice cream sandwiches are always popular "carry-around-as-you-shop" items. Hot coffee, lemonade and bottled soft-drinks are essential.

Don't forget in the center of all the excitement to serve those ears of corn you've been so well publicizing. Steam them well, dip in butter and serve on a stick!

Now, here's the recipe for Coney Dogs:

Coney Dogs (160 servings)

2¼ quarts flour	1 tablespoon salt
4½ cups cornmeal	6 eggs, beaten
3 tablespoons baking powder	5¼ cups milk
¾ cup sugar	160 frankfurters

Combine first five ingredients. Blend eggs and milk. Mix with dry ingredients. Wipe frankfurters. Dip in mixture.

Deep fat fry. Stand on end in pan to drain. Serve on hot-dog buns with lots of catsup available!

Parties for Mental Health

Don't *you* like to go to parties? Don't *you* like to wake up in the morning and think, "Hooray—this is going to be a *good* day, I can hardly wait for the party tonight!"

Patients in mental hospitals feel the same way, except, perhaps, more so, since they have so few happy, exciting experiences to look forward to.

The Director of Volunteer Services at Galesburg Research Hospital in Galesburg, Illinois, chatted with me in a most informative way so that these party ideas could be shared with you. Galesburg Research Hospital is a government owned and operated institution with more than 1400 mental patients located in a city of 37,000 population. Volunteers come primarily from within a fifteen mile radius of the hospital.

Although these suggestions have come specifically from central Illinois, the ideas have been offered to whet *your* imagination and ingenuity, so that you can inquire in your community as to what can be done most effectively there. There are undoubtedly many overlapping suggestions—the guitar playing and listening enthusiasm sweeping the nation is surely no less popular in New Jersey, Texas or Colorado than in the mid-west.

INVITATIONS: The term "invitations" is being used loosely, because the patients do not receive individual invitations to the party, but do attend in a group accompanied by their own ward nurses and attendants.

176

The term "invitations" is retained, however, to emphasize the importance of regular parties. It is suggested that a sponsoring group be assigned one ward of the mental hospital and that each month the group plan a party for this same ward. In this way, the patients get to know the volunteers personally and look forward to the same people coming back, as we would look forward to a reunion with old friends. The patients remember the names of the volunteers who come monthly and their regular return brings those in the hospital a thread of continuity with the outside world.

Club, church, homemakers' or other groups may agree to sponsor bi-monthly parties, but the monthly program or event at Research Hospital is the one most desired and most helpful to the patients.

TRAINING: Party giving at a mental hospital is somewhat different than inviting your neighbors in for coffee. There are certain rules and goals and directions in which this institutional party ought to go.

To explain this program, day or half-day In-service training is given each fall by trained therapists. The public is cordially invited to attend, and handcraft and game ideas are given which may also be used in working with those in nursing homes or other special situations.

Young people, fifteen and sixteen years of age, may serve as summer Junior Volunteers and at this period the girls wear candy striped uniforms and the young men wear blue coats provided by the Research Hospital.

Passing out books or booklets to be read at home concerning the work and rules of volunteer service has not proved satisfactory, since the books are usually not read on an independent basis and frequently not returned.

FUN: The best volunteers encourage patients to produce their own programs—perhaps of simple skits or jokes and singing that they can lead and participate in themselves.

Travelogs

Travelogs and slide programs produced by volunteers are appreciated by patients. Remember the movies you made of last year's vacation that your neighbors ignored and your friends dozed through? Here is a place where they *will* be appreciated, *if* you go along with them and make the program an interesting one by the sharing of your own personality. Be sincere and carry a happy, party attitude with you for contagious fun.

Musical Programs

If you are willing to share your piano-playing or song leading talent, the patients in a mental hospital will respond enthusiastically. Favorite programs are those made up and created by the volunteers themselves for this special party occasion.

A very favorite current program is *guitar playing*. Patients are delighted by guitar music and often the sons and daughters of adult volunteers will come with their parents to help put on this kind of a party when they understand the real need for "fun" that a hospital patient has.

Reading and Poetry Programs

"But I can't dance or sing or play the guitar or even the piano." This is no excuse. You can read poetry or a funny story. Patients are pleased just because you have come to see them. Your Woman's Club group may think your jokes are corny and your family think you can scarcely read a newspaper let alone tell a funny story, but ward patients will think you are marvelous. This feeling is extremely good for one's own self-esteem—just try it and see!

Sports

This is popular, particularly in men's wards, but the most necessary requirement is that you play along with the patients.

They don't want just to watch you, and they certainly don't want you to watch them, but if you can join in the familiar games that they already know, this is excellent. Check with the Department of Volunteer Services at your nearest Mental Hospital and probably most of the sports equipment is there, waiting for you to come and use it *with* the patients. Here are some Galesburg favorite sports or recreation areas:

> Table tennis
> Volley Ball
> Ring toss
> Folk dancing
> Croquet

GAMES

Patients like the old favorites that they know well and are familiar with the rules such as:

> Musical Chairs
> Pin the Tail on the Donkey
> Bingo (the service veterans particularly like this)
> Scrabble

Another suggestion which has been well received is to cut out advertisements or other pictures into two sections and have the patients, or guests as they certainly are at this party hour, match the pieces with one another and with those who have come in the group from outside to play the games with them.

They might also match name tags, but prior to this it is important that volunteers wear name tags so they can be easily identified by the patients and called by name.

FAVORS: Holiday favors are very popular with the patients and these can be varied, of course, for almost any time of the year. Besides the usual Hallowe'en and Christmas, they are delighted to make May Day baskets or Fourth of July paper rockets or cherry trees for George Washington's birthday.

Patients are delighted to make their own favors, but it is important that most of these projects be fairly well assembled before they are brought to the hospital, so that only the last finishing touches need to be added by those at the party. It is important not to frustrate the patients with complicated directions or things that are too involved for them to grasp easily. A May Day basket might be assembled with the bows to be added at the hospital and perhaps some artificial flowers tucked in by those in the wards.

Regressive patients particularly need to feel they have really accomplished something and attractive favors to which they can add extra beauty touches are a real boost to their morale.

FOOD: Of course, patients like to eat and they are delighted with homemade food, but the policy of the hospital is to play down the emphasis on food and to emphasize the entertainment of the party.

Homemade cookies are particularly welcome at the parties, however, and the hospital will provide either coffee or punch to go with the cookies which the volunteers bring to the wards.

Cookies are particularly welcome because dishes and silverware are not necessary when they are served, and so the preparation in the hospital is less complicated than, for instance, blueberry pie a la mode!

Here are two recipes that should please both the patients with the flavors and hospital staff with the ease in serving.

PEANUT COOKIES

¾ cup soft shortening
½ cup granulated sugar
1 cup firmly packed brown sugar
2 eggs
1 teaspoon vanilla
1½ cups sifted all-purpose flour
½ teaspoon salt
½ teaspoon soda
1 cup salted peanuts
2 cups Quaker Oats (quick or old-fashioned, uncooked)

Beat shortening, sugars, eggs and vanilla together until creamy. Sift together flour, salt and soda. Add to creamed mixture, blending well. Stir in peanuts and oats. Drop by heaping teaspoonfuls onto ungreased cooky sheets. Bake in preheated moderate oven—375 degrees for 12 to 15 minutes. Makes 4 dozen.

CRUNCHY PICNIC CANDY

5 cups Quaker Cap'n Crunch cereal	⅓ cup peanut butter
4 cups miniature marshmallows	¼ cup butter or margarine
	½ cup semi-sweet chocolate pieces

Pour Cap'n Crunch into large greased bowl. Melt marshmallows, peanut butter, and butter in top of double boiler over hot water, stirring occasionally until smooth. Pour over cereal, stirring until evenly coated.

With greased hands, shape to form fifteen three inch round patties. Place on waxed paper. Melt chocolate pieces in top of double boiler over hot, not boiling water. Spread the center of each patty with chocolate. Refrigerate until set. Makes fifteen patties.

Novel Nursing Home Fun

Probably few institutions in the United States have made as fine advancements in buildings and procedures in the last decade as have nursing homes. Contemporary buildings, bright, gay rooms, able nursing care, physical therapists, balanced and special diets prepared in remarkably clean kitchens—this is the new, carefully inspected nursing home—a far cry from some unfortunate relics of a generation ago.

There is a wholesome and pleasant atmosphere in this new environment and a good portion of our community may find themselves part of it at some period of their lives. Not only is it the very old who are part of nursing homes today, but young people as well, recuperating from surgery or with permanent disabilities, such as the quadraplegic. In these new homes there is planned recreation, regular physical therapy and most administrators would like to have still more recreation and more parties, too.

Most homes will welcome volunteer groups from the community who will come in and supervise a party for the patients who are able to be out of their beds, either ambulatory people or those in wheelchairs.

INVITATIONS: The invitations essentially go to you, the volunteers who are the concerned people of the community and who are aware of those in nursing homes. You are needed to share with these patients your enthusiasm, your talents and your party spirit.

Party enthusiasm is contagious. Bring it with you and share it. It is amazing how an invitation to fun can spark happiness in those with illnesses, problems and disabilities (not that we don't *all* have problems; it's just that theirs are a little more so).

Parties given in a nursing home situation can turn out to be some of the most satisfying that you have ever planned. Be sure to check in detail with the administrator of your local home before you order volley balls or candy bars. Those in wheelchairs could not use the volley balls, nor the diabetics eat the candy. Party props will need to be chosen with care!

If a nursing home in your area does invite you to have a party, try very hard to keep the date you have selected. Those who live outside their own homes count on special parties and are more disappointed than busy, active people when a special treat has to be cancelled.

DECORATIONS: A friend told me about visiting an aunt on her eightieth birthday. Since the birthday lady was not able to be out of her bed, her niece strung eight tea bags on a line across the bottom of the bed—for a happy Eight-Tea Birthday, you see!

Wrap individual life savers or bright colored gumdrops in clear plastic wrap and tie each one to a small jewelry tree to decorate a bedside table. This doesn't have to be for Christmas. You might use pink mints for a spring party to represent cherry blossoms with a wee bit of pink and green crepe paper attached to the mints.

Another aspect of *Decorations* might be the props which go with the games or recreation you are planning for the nursing home. These need not necessarily be the traditional streamers that take a long time to hang and loop correctly, but in this case, the decorations are the items needed in the games you plan to play.

For instance, if you plan to have the mock fishing contest and you leave at home the rubber bobbers, there will be a great deal of disappointment. If you forget the prizes or the harmonica you planned to play for the Sing-Out, this disrupts the spirit of the party. Make a list and remember to check off needed equipment, as you pack the car or box or purse!

FUN: Remember that people are different and that different nursing homes have different kinds of people so that one party may be enthusiastically received in one place yet go over like a limp dishcloth in another because of the interest of the patients or their abilities.

Here are some activities that were planned for a Fourth of July party in the midwest for those who were able to go outside to the courtyard to participate:

BEACH-VOLLEY BALL

A net was set up and a lightweight plastic beach ball was used instead of a volley ball. Inside, this might be done with a clothesline and balloons.

PUTTING CONTEST

Golf clubs can be loaned to the patients and that they may enjoy a putting contest with practice balls. Remember that the party must be geared to a much slower pace and care taken that the patients not over-exert themselves.

SACK RACE

When hearing of this, I was aghast at the thought of elderly and invalid people with their legs in burlap potato bags trying to hop along. This *isn't* what the name implies.

(The difficulty comes because I was raised in Philadelphia where a brown paper container was a "bag," but here in Illinois this same paper container is not a "bag" but a "sack." So, this is a brown paper "sack" relay and one doesn't put one's feet in them anyhow, at least not in this race.)

Five persons on one team might compete against five persons on the other side. Each team is given *two* paper sacks—one for each team containing ten similar or identical articles.

At the signal to begin, the first person on each team takes out one item at a time from one "sack" and puts it into the other one. When the ten items have been transferred, both bags are given to the next person in line for a repetition of the same procedure.

Whichever team is able to transfer and re-transfer the items first, wins the game. This could be continued by having the patients write down as many of the articles as they can remember from the "sack."

For relays and other games which suggest prizes, patients may be allowed their choice of an item from a large bowl of fruit. Candy is not suggested since some of the guests may be diabetic or others on diets where candy and sugars are limited.

Don't plan any games, especially active ones, without the permission of the administrator or director of physical therapy for the home. Some of the activities suggested might be too strenuous for all the patients in a particular place.

Here are some other possibilities for you and your committee to consider in planning these parties, however.

FISHING CONTEST

In warm weather a children's wading pool might be set up in the yard, patio or courtyard with those able to participate casting their lines with rubber bobbers attached. If the bobber is thrown into the wading pool, someone stationed there, puts a plastic fish on the bobber. Each fish may have a number attached and the contestants add up their numbers (supposedly the weight of the fish) at the end of the Fishing Tournament. If possible the winner of the fishing contest might be taken on a real fishing trip, even a brief one, if it is feasable health-wise and lake-wise. In any case an inexpensive but seemingly elaborate "trophy" is awarded him for his angling skill!

"I TOOK A TRIP . . ."

This game, too, is played differently, not in its usual pattern of taking things along in alphabetical order. In this version the patient begins by saying, "I took a trip to _____" and adds *any* letter of the alphabet.

The rest of the guests may guess *K*alamazoo or *K*ansas for K and *I*reland, *I*ndiana, *I*celand or *I*ndianapolis for I. The first guest to call out the name of the place that the caller had in mind, may himself begin the game again by saying "I took a trip to _____" with a different initial.

The game may get complicated when two letters are called. At one nursing home party the letters EP were called out. Some guessed Estes Park, but no one came up with the answer the patient had in mind—*E*ast *P*eoria.

Another variation is to say: "My father owns a grocery store and he sells _____." Here again the initial is inserted, but this time it stands for items like *C*ake, *C*abbage, *C*orn, *C*offee, or *C*ookies, if the letter given is C.

SPELLING BEES

These are popular with many ages.

GROUP EXERCISES

After checking with the physical therapist, mild ones, including folk games might be done slowly to some light and whimsical recorded music.

DEMONSTRATIONS

If you have a button collection or have an assortment of dolls from different countries, you will be the delight of many nursing home parties. One lady shared her collection of cameos and told the history of them while another guest demonstrated her hobby of china painting and showed her cups and plates with pink and yellow roses gracefully handpainted on them.

Hobbies like arrowhead collecting, leather tooling or ceramics are all popular when shared in the nursing home party situation. You will find your own hobby expanded and enriched by the interest and appreciation of those with whom you share.

COMMUNITY SING

Don't necessarily look for the *best* soprano to lead singing at the nursing home. The person needed is someone who can get the patients to join in. If the singer is too perfect, the music will turn into a solo with the guests just *listening*.

If it's a Group Sing you're having, you want everyone to join in. Have several persons mingle with the patients, because as voices come from different places in the room, those in the Home will feel encouraged to join and express their feelings in their old favorite songs.

FAVORS: Patients love these, especially when they are brought by Brownies, Scouts, 4-H groups or other children and young people whom the oldsters enjoy seeing. They like the favors already made up and many patients cherish small favors and keep them for many months.

Almost anyone could make and send a favor, couldn't they? Here is one favor which some Girl Scout troops have made.

Rose Paperweight

Materials needed: 6 inch strip of nylon net (whatever width it comes in—usually 72 inches)
1 small baby food jar
1 plastic flower
Art foam or felt (padding for bottom)
Rubber band
Colored water

Squeeze flower gently together and put in baby food jar upside down. Fill with colored water and put lid on tightly. Glue a piece of art foam or felt across the lid, as this will be the base of the favor and you don't want to scratch table or bureau.

Fold net in half lengthwise. Gather with running stitch on folded edge and draw up to approximate size of jar. Put a rubber band between the two layers and fit around jar.

Artificial holly and red or green net might be used at the Christmas season with perhaps an artificial rose and pastel net for a spring or summer favor.

FOOD: Again, as in the parties for other institutions and for young children, keep it simple. These patients are as enthused as children and they will be happiest with uncomplicated refreshments. Here is a possible menu:

> Peach Ice Cream (homemade or otherwise)
> Vanilla Cookies   Orangeade

A favor might be an orange gumdrop with a small artificial flag or flower stuck in the center. Cover the gumdrop with clear plastic wrap, so the favor may be kept on a bedside table or bureau as a remembrance of the party.

Index